SHOVELS OF GLORY

DAVID FITZGERALD

CONTENTS

Introduction

This book is based on my recollections of growing up in Hillsboro Oregon. I have avoided many of the negative events that occurred instead leaning on the happier moments. The names were all changed of those still living so as to not cause any distress to those individuals.

This book will most likely be considered fiction since it is based entirely on my recollection of events. From my perspective these events did occur and are true. While I have a good memory for events, perspective can have a profound impact on the memories of other people witnessing the same event. I have guessed my age for the events and believe them to be Ball Park accurate.

I wrote this book at the prompting of friends and family who enjoyed my stories about growing up in a small town with a neighborhood dominated by boys. Why so many boys? For now I will assume it was mere chance. Please read this book with a light heart even though it represents growing up in the 1960's and 1970's under the ever present nuclear threat and the cold war.

My father who played a prominent role in my upbringing was born in Vermont and passed away in 2009 from liver disease that he brought home while serving in the army during the Korean War. During the war he was a staff sergeant on an engineering platoon. The first of my paternal grandparents children were born in 1918 during World War One. All of my father's seven brothers and sisters have passed away as of this writing.

My Mother was born in Vermont and is still living. Her and her small dog Squirt live in the Rocky Mountains enjoying retirement and having occasional dinners at Denny's. All of her brothers and sisters except for two are still living near the small Vermont village where they were born.

I and my brother were born in Pasadena California but moved to Oregon before we were two years old. Both of my parents worked outside of the home, my father as a machinist and my mother as a legal secretary. This was not the norm at the time but was becoming increasingly necessary. We were latch key children during an age when a child alone for a few hours after school was considered safe. I do remember that we had to be well behaved so as to avoid being caught by neighborhood mothers. They were only too happy to discuss our transgressions with our parents.

CHAPTER 1

The Early Years

My parents both grew up in the Morrisville Vermont area where they lived on dairy farms. After returning from the Korean war an army sergeant Dad began courting his future wife. At the same time Dad worked odd jobs as a farm hand, ski lodge kitchen assistant, grooming ski slopes and repairing farm equipment and automobiles.

My Grandmother considered Dad an undesirable, so when Dad stopped to pick Mom up for a date Grandmother chased him from the house using a broom and would have beat him senseless if she could have caught him. Many years later Dad made it up to grandmother by renovating her bathroom and replacing her flooring. Not to be dissuaded, Mom and Dad married in 1954 in Wolcott Vermont. Wolcott was a very small village of 700 souls 10 miles from Morrisville. Jobs in the area were hard to come by but after working for a spell in the asbestos mines Dad work as mechanic. Mom worked part time as a secretary for a local attorney.

By 1957 they were fed up with the poor job prospects and lured by the riches of California packed up their VW Beetle and started for Los Angeles. Mom was pregnant at the time with me and vividly remembers crossing the hot arid stretches of Arizona with the heater on full blast to prevent the car from overheating.

They ended up in Pasadena California where Dad went to work for the Edsel dealership as a mechanic. In December 1957 my paternal grandfather passed away in Vermont at age 62. He died following a simple cataract surgery due to a blood clot.

In 1958 at the Huntington Hospital in Pasadena I was born. We lived over a detached garage in a single room apartment but soon moved into a small home. A little over a year later my brother was born in the same hospital.

The Edsel job did not work out well for Dad and Mom took part time work as a secretary again. Discouraged and still struggling they heard from Dad's brother Uncle Don and his wife Aunt Sue who lived in Hillsboro Oregon that there were lots of great jobs. Uncle Don and Aunt Sue had moved to Oregon a few years earlier from Vermont and were the only other ones to have moved out of the state of Vermont.

Don and Sue painted a rosy picture of good jobs and inexpensive housing. They had three children at the time, there youngest two years older than I. The decision was made and we moved from Pasadena to Hillsboro. We rented the farm house on the Hawthorne farms. The house faced busy Cornell Road and was surrounded by wheat fields. Today this is the location of an Intel corporate facility.

Dad got a job in Newberg as a mechanic and Mom got a job in Beaverton as a legal secretary. During this time Dad decided to make a change and went to machinist school while still working for the Chevrolet dealer. He eventually took a job in Gresham working for the Cascade

Corporation where he remained for 25 years. He made the 36 mile trip from Hillsboro to Fairview every day travelling through Portland on surface streets before the freeways were completed.

The house on Hawthorne farms was a simple farm house, un-insulated and drafty. A single gas stove in the center of the living room provided the only heat for the house. This is where my brother and I went through measles, chicken pox and mumps. The house across the street our closest neighbors had a German shepherd they let run loose and forced us to play inside on most days until his days ended on the busy street.

With both parents away they hired a sweet older woman that we knew as Grammy Nichols. Grammy was Grandmother to us and was a part of our lives for many years. She lived to be 103 years old.

One day I decided the best place to ride my trike was inside the house. I drug it up the front steps and through the front door where I was greeted by Grammy who used her broom to sweep me gentle out the door.

During the years on Hawthorne farms we had a black and white TV with three stations. My brother and I watched Captain Kangaroo with his friend Mr. Green Jeans. My brother was a fan of Mr. Bunny Rabbit. To this day he carries a rabbit's foot to remember him by. There was also Rusty Nails the clown and Ramblin' Rod. Rod had a TV show with a bleacher full of kids, we both wanted to go on the show but never had the chance. Years later I took my own children and had a chance to talk with him for a bit. He was an extremely nice man and a credit to the Portland Oregon area.

I also loved to watching Sky King the flying constable played by Kirby Grant. One fall Mr. Grant came to Hillsboro and appeared at the armory. The place was packed with parents and children but he took time to talk with each child and sign a photograph. My Father made me stay in the bleachers until the last person left, I was sure I was going to miss out. When everyone had left Dad took me down to see Mr. Grant. It was quiet and he spent a half hour talking with my father. I still have a picture of him taken at the armory that day along with my love for airplanes.

1962 brought me to my first day of Kindergarten. The bus picked me up in front of the house and we drove to Peter Boscow elementary school on 3rd street in Hillsboro. My teacher was Mrs. Joyce, she was fond of snow skiing and proved it by returning from Christmas break with a wheel chair and two broken legs. The kids in class provided the power to move her chair when she needed assistance.

Kindergarten wasn't much of a challenge as I could already read and print my letters. The day we received our first book I finished reading it while they were still being passed out. My favorite subject was nap time, while most kids fidgeted and whispered I was out like a light.

The next summer I went running in the back yard barefoot where I found a piece of broken glass by stepping on it. I hobbled over to where Dad was working and held up my foot now covered in blood. Dad didn't believe in doctors, he grew up on a farm where you did everything your-self. His first remedy was antiseptic powder and his second was hydrogen peroxide. Dad's eyes bulged at the site of all the blood, he swept me up in his arms and into the house where he doused my foot hydrogen peroxide and wrapped it in a towel. He stuck me in the woody station wagon then whisked me off to the doctor's office.

Why the doctor's office and not emergency room? Today we have emergency rooms and clinics in nearly every town but in the 1960's there were no emergency clinics and the hospital's emergency services were dramatically different then they are today.

The second event of the summer occurred in Mom's old car along Baseline road in Beaverton. The old car had no seat belts and since we couldn't see out the window sitting we were kneeling on the front seat. An intoxicated man ran a stop sign and T-boned Mom's car, my brother and I were thrown to the floor and fortunately not through the windshield. I remember looking up from the floor board and wondering how I got there.

Mom and Dad purchased a small ranch style home on Forest street in Hillsboro Oregon and we moved into town. There were lots of kids in the neighborhood and school was only three blocks away. This was the start of another era and a whole new set of challenges.

CHAPTER 2

The Storm

We moved to Oregon in 1960 and lived in the farm house that occupied the old Hawthorne farms. Two years later we experienced the worst storm to hit the Pacific Northwest in its recorded history. Before hitting the Pacific coast the storm was Typhoon Freda. The winds of the storm had several reports of 145 miles per hour the Mount Hebo radar station located 10 miles from the Oregon coast reported winds of 170 miles per hour. The storm caused millions of dollars in damage and caused extensive power outages road blockages for weeks.

At the time of the storm our baby sitter was a kindly older woman named Winnie Nichols that we referred to as Grandma Nichols. She was the heart of hospitality and good will and our anchor during the storm. She was in and out of our lives for many years until her death at 103 years old in the early 1990s.

On the day of the storm I must have had a premonition, I decided to drag my tricycle up the front steps of the Hawthorne farms house and into the living room. But alas that was not to be, Grandma Nichols gently swept me from the house with tricycle in tow. A few hours later it started to become dark and Grandma brought us boys into the house. She was apprehensive and continuously peeked out the windows. In the back ground the radio played the news while my brother and I played on the living room floor.

Before the wind struck Grandma brought blankets from the bedrooms and covered the windows in the living room to prevent broken glass from flying into the room. She then secured all the windows and doors, peeked out the front window one more time and said a prayer to God. She then very calmly went to the kitchen and prepared tomato soup over our gas stove. We ate and it became darker, and then darker still as evening came on.

The wind started to howl and the three of us huddled on the couch covered by blankets in the living room. The light in the living room stayed on for a while but then blinked out. Prepared, she lit candles so that we would not be completely in the dark. The time for Mom and Dad to be home had come and gone and though I didn't know it at the time Grandma Nichols was shaking with fear. To us boys she appears calm as she read to us out loud raising her voice as the wind howled.

Then there came a crash from my bedroom, before she could stop me I was up in a flash. Opening the bedroom door I saw our picnic table lying across my bed. Grandma snatch me back and shut the door. The wind continue to howl and we kept hearing crashing and banging from far and near.

Eventually I dozed off as any four year old might. When I opened my eyes Mom and Dad were there and it was quiet outside as the winds had died down. Dad left with Grandma Nichols to take her home. Many years later Grandma related how terrifying the trip home had been. They had to repeatedly cross downed trees and walk across downed power lines to make it the half mile back to where Dad had left his car. They then spent two hours to travel the 5 miles back to her home stopping and turning around frequently to find a path.

The day after the storm Mom and Dad didn't go to work. Mom worked as a legal secretary in Beaverton and Dad as a machinist in Gresham. With no power at their employers there was no reason to go. We had heat and our stove worked thanks to NW Natural Gas. It would take weeks before everything was back to normal.

Dad took me outside with him the next day and we searched the property around the house and looked out across the barren fields. Everything was swept clean, the fence was gone and my play house were not to be seen as far as the eye could see. The trike I had attempted to save was gone never to be seen again. We walked down the road toward the horse barns where we saw large trees across the road and spoke with some of the neighbors.

When we returned home Dad pulled out his chain saw and sharpened the teeth. Then with the saw and a can of gas we walked back down Cornell road to the horse barns. Along with several large trees the were numerous downed power lines but the power to the area was out and would remain so for several weeks.

Dad set me up on a large tree trunk where I ran back and forth between the branches. He took his chain saw and started to cut down through the tree. When he stopped I ran back to see that he had not quite cut through the center of the tree. He moved down the tree to cut through from the same side again only reaching halfway through. Eventually he balanced the saw on top of the tree and crossed to the other side. When he finished there were still a chunk of tree between the cuts that required using a cross-cut saw. Eventually a neighbor showed up and between them they started to make some real progress.

Eventually a neighbor showed up with a tractor to move the logs but they still spent five days clearing the road in both directions before Dad could get his car back into the driveway.

Grandma Nichols and I talked about the storm many years later when I was an adult and she in her 90s. She said it was the scariest night of her life and she shook every minute through the whole ordeal. You would never have known the night of the storm that she feared anything accept God. She was the rock that kept me calm through the storm.

CHAPTER 3

To Know my Father

A key and important figure to all that is to follows is my Father or as we referred to him "Dad", the neighborhood boys called him Mr. Fitzgerald, as well as the Boy Scouts in the troop where he was assistant scoutmaster. There are a few details some of you may find alarming in today's culture but were in fact quite common at the time. My father while tough, a grouch and at times rough was never discriminatory or bigoted.

My father Gerald was born in 1930 on a farm in Northern Vermont, blue eyes and blond hair, the apple of his Mothers eye. He was the seventh child and 5 boy of what would eventually become 8 children. His parents were also born in Vermont in Lake Elmore and interesting enough within the same year 1895. The farm was purchased by Grandfather 1918, this included a farm house located on a gravel road. Across the road was the equipment barn and attached small horse barn. The center of activity on the farm was the dairy barn adjunct to the equipment barn.

The cow barn had a large main floor with head stalls for holding the Holstein dairy cows while milking. Above the cows was the loft used to store hay and grain that was needed to sustain the cows and there calves through the long cold Vermont winters. It was not unusual for the cows to spend several weeks in the barn if the weather was very cold. During these time everyone worked hard to keep the stalls cleaned and the cows contented.

Attached to the barn was a small room called the milking parlor, this contained a large 500 gallon stainless steel vessel to store the milk gathered each morning and evening. Each morning sometime after the early milking the large truck from the dairy would come by and drain the tank, this would then need to be clean and sanitized before the next milking.

The property extended to either side of the road gently sloping with the road. All told 137 acres of pasture and trees. Along the road to either side was a loose stone wall built over many years from all the stones that the frost heaved up in the pastures and fields. This is a familiar site in upstate Vermont

From the house across the road, past the machine shed, over a small brook and pasture there was an orchard of Sugar Maple trees. Nestled in these trees was a sugar house, this is a house where sap from the trees is processed. Each year when the temperatures drop below freezing and again raise above freezing during the day the sap flows and needs to be gathered. Grandfather and all his children would traipse through the trees, drilling holes, inserting spigots and hanging buckets from the hook on the spigot. The syrup captured in the spigot was then carried to the Sugar house, poured into a large shallow pan then boiled to remove excess water and make maple syrup.

This was important to the livelihood of the farm as the maple syrup was boiled by grandmother in to sugar for use in baking and cooking. In a good years excess was sold to neighbors as well as stores in town.

The children including my father lived on the products of the farm that included milk a few steers, eggs, chickens, a vegetable garden canned and put away each year. They also had milk in plenty after large quantities were sold to the local bottler.

Dad was the next to youngest out of eight children for many years, the very last boy came 8 years after my father so in his mind he was the youngest in the family. Dad once told me that he resented his youngest brother coming along so late and consuming all of his mother's affections.

The chores on farm never end, and once completed started anew. Seven boys and girls can get into a lot of mischief so Grandfather was forced to keep them working every minute they weren't in school.

One nice spring day Grandfather set all the kids to white washing the outside of the barn. Once finished he put them to work cleaning and white washing the inside of the barn. No one knows quite how things start but it can be assumed that one brother looked up and saw the back of his sister's head and next to the bucket that he was dipping his brush in was a nearly fresh green ball of manure. Well the temptation would prove to great and soon with great hand eye coordination splattered into the back off her head.

Sister put her hand up and felt the greasy messy now trickling down her back. At this she turned in hopes of spotting the culprit, but much to her dismay everyone was busy with their bucket and brush. She then determined to go on the war path, picking up her bucket shed exited the barn but was soon back with a large bucket of ammunition from the manure pile. She then vented her wrath upon the offender who in her mind was everyone else in the barn.

In no time at all there was a seven sided war. The manure leaping from young hands to strike sister and brother alike with the additional bonus that missiles missing there intended target splashed against the white washed walls. Up to this point a good time was being had by all and they laughed out loud at each successful strike.

It was into this carnage that Grandfather stepped. He was never known to be overly kind or patient, indeed he was known for his volatile temper. He also never just stepped quietly into a room and in this case he exploded venting his wrath immediately on the participants. The manure war ended almost as quickly as it started.

Grandfather using his loudest voiced told everyone to stand where they were. He exist the barn but returned within minutes with a good stiff willow switch. It took no time at all and there were seven very sore backsides. No explanation was requested and none required but each in there turn screamed out there innocence. When next he stepped from the barn there were seven sore back sides cleaning and again white washing.

To better understand the mind of my Grandfather and the environment that my father grew up in is best related by a story from my father's older brother: One day Hugh, Dad's older brother was trying out his new BB gun. He was feeling very confident and visualize himself quite the marksman. While thus engaged his father, my grandfather stepped out onto the back porch of the house. Thinking his father to far away to be struck, He swept the BB gun to his shoulder and carelessly fired off a round towards Grandfather. The BB founds it mark in the corner of Grandfathers eye. You probable agree with me that his could not possible go unpunished.

Hugh quickly ran the options through his mind, run and never come back or face the music. Neither was much of a choice and as these thoughts churned through his young mind Grandfather turned and spied

Hugh and only Hugh with his BB gun. Grandfather gently took the BB gun from Hugh's hands and with a motion of his hand directed him towards the wood shed. While at the wood shed waiting for his father's return, Hugh found himself with time to contemplate what he had done and to dread what was coming. It was at this moment that a brilliant plan arose. He would break all the small sticks into little pieces and hide all the sticks too big to break. In this way his Father would be unable to spank him and have to be satisfied with a stern lecture. Implementing his plan he sat back to await Grandfather.

Through the window of the wood shed Hugh spied father, in Grandfather's hand was a thick black rubber milking hose. Needless to say punishment was administered and lesson learned. Hugh would later go on to be one of the many soldiers that fought on Iwo Jima during the Second World War and unlike many others return home again.

On one fateful day my father along with his next oldest brother Don and the neighbor kid found they had time on their hands, this did not often occur on the farm so a replacement activity was called for.

Slipping into the house they took Grandfather's old rifle a muzzle loader and a bag of gun powder with the thought of trying out the old gun. The black power used in these old guns is not as powerful as that used in modern bullet cartridges. Modern guns use high speed gun powder witch burns much faster and hotter providing greater force then a similar amount of black powder. What they did not know was that they had Grandfathers high speed powder.

They took the gun across the road and down to the far bottom of the pasture where they could not be seen from the house. They then started filling the gun with high speed powder and rocks. The gun was not quite full and looking around they found some nails near the fence left over. They filled the old gun clear to the top careful to tamp it down firmly as they went.

It was now time to fire the gun, Dad and Don refused to do it, but neighbor kid always anxious to prove himself brave volunteered for the duty. He stood with his back to a large tree and slowly pulled the gun up with both arms, it was too heavy to hold against his arm so he let the stock wrest against his sternum. At the last minute as he was preparing to pull the trigger everyone had second thoughts. Looking around they were able to prop the gun up onto forked sticks and leaned it against the tree. Then using a long stick they set it off.

There was a deafening explosion and huge flash, the boys were temporarily knocked senseless and onto their backs. Once there eyes started to recover and they pulled themselves back to their feet they turned to examine the gun. The wood stock was split from the barrel and the metal of the barrel was pealed back like a banana. There was no doubt in any of their minds that the gun would never fire again. But the most shocking outcome was yet to be found. Looking at the tree there was a mass of rocks and nails imbedded into the trunk as big as Dad's hand. Recently I spoke with Uncle Don about the event and he related that he was really glad that at the last moment the decision to not hold the gun was made. I then told him on my last trip to Vermont that I had found the same from tree they used 75 years ago and you could still see the mass of rocks and nails in the tree.

Dad finished the eighth grade and did not return but continued to work on the farm. Eventually he took on odd jobs in Stowe working for a ski lodge. This provided extra money that was usually expended on cars and girls.

At 18 years old Dad enlisted into the US Army eventually reaching the rank of Staff Sargent heading a platoon of men tasked with engineering projects that included building roads, bridges, disarming mind fields and bobby traps. The platoon was all black, that is of Afro-American descent, only my father was of white or European descent and if they had known one quarter Native American. It was a shocking truth to my young father that even during the Korean War that your life could be limited by color of your skin. He was determined to treat his men no differently and supported them in their efforts to the best of his abilities. For the remainder of his life he lived a life that shouted, all men are equal, they need only prove themselves on their own merit and not on their back ground. During my formative years we were always expected to act respectfully and treat all adults with proper manners.

Before leaving Korea Dad was offered a position as a drill sergeant when he re-enlisted. Dad decided to return home where he found to work in the asbestos mines. His job was to walk the conveyer belt and knock free debris on the rollers therefore allowing the belt to move smoothly. This was not very pleasant work and eventually he found work assisting in the local repair shop working on cars and trucks.

He met my Mother who was 5 years his junior, then he met my Mother's Mother. The first time Dad showed up at the house Grandmother chased him back into the yard with a broom and let him know in no uncertain terms that he was not welcome. Eventually they were married.

Dad continued to work as a mechanic and Mom found work in a legal office in their small town. The pay was low and the hours short. Additionally there was no room to advance and improve.

They decided to try California as there was a shortage of jobs in Vermont. They drove Pasadena California in there 1952 VW Bug. They had never had a honeymoon so they made the trip an adventure stopping Washington DC and then at many other sites down across the south western united states. The heat was challenging for the car as well as to my pregnant Mother. The cars heater had to remain on all the time to cool the car while Mom suffered the heat and pregnancy.

While in California I was born then a little over a year later my younger brother. Dad found work at a new Edsel dealership as an auto mechanic. Our stay was shorter than the life of the Edsel witch lasted less than 3 years.

At my Uncle Don's prompting, the same one as in the muzzle loader incident above. We bundled everything in our old woody Chevrolet wagon and headed North for Oregon and settled in Hillsboro Oregon. Mom found work as a legal secretary and Dad decided to train as a machinist.

Oregon is where my early memories begin; with no memories of California. I have always considered Oregon to be my one and only home.

Dad passed away a few years ago but in the stories related here you will experience some of his life and much of mine growing up in Hillsboro Oregon.

CHAPTER 4

Building the Family Room

The family room was a great addition for our home. It placed the TV and kids in a separate room so that Mom and Dad could entertain guests in the living room. Then when my parents started a pinochle party it gave them lots of room for the three tables they needed and still allowed them the kitchen table to array snacks and drinks.

One day during my summer vacation I was wandering around outside and walked back to our small backyard. I saw where someone had been chipping away at the concrete patio and had left evidence in the form of a sledge hammer and pry bar. I thought at first my brother had been up to mischief but a few minutes later he came looking for me and at that point categorically denied any involvement. Both of us knew there would be a whipping involved if either of us were involved.

At this point while looking at the patio and tools that we both came to the same conclusion, Dad wants this torn up! Exchanging glances we each choose our implement of destruction and started pounding away at the patio. Now this was fun and thrilling, smashing things is much more fun then building and we dug in with gusto.

It wasn't long before Tony, my brother's friend showed up and wanted to know what was going on. We brought Tony up to date on the plan after which he ran home and returned with a hammer. I quite lost track of time, but looking around I could see that we were making slow progress. The concrete was old, hard and thick.

I paused at this point to reflect and with dread realized I didn't know if this was really what Dad wanted done. Fear slowly crept in and I could feel the shivers along my spine as the hairs on my neck rose. I knew what the consequences would be. These thoughts quickly fled as two more neighbor kids showed up with hammers and shovels. Soon another boy brought his father's sledge hammer and we really started to make progress.

Sun started to sink as evening approached, while 8 kids industriously pounded away at the concrete. It was at this point that I looked up at all of the kids and one adult. Unknown to me my father had shown up still in his work uniform. He stood glaring at us with that look I had dreaded earlier. Dad approached Mickey and with a smile and showed him how to run the wrecking bar deep under a slab of concrete and pry up a giant piece of the concrete. With Dad's help we soon had all the pieces pried loose and broken up.

Dad then hooked up the trailer to the truck and we quickly loaded the chunks of concrete and excess dirt and sod. All of the boys piled into the truck bed for the journey to the nearby land fill. We were quite a site hanging over the sides of the truck and shouting at other kids we passed. During the return journey Dad swung into North Side Grocery where each of us was allowed to get one soda and one treat. The final leg of our journey was quieter as we each slurped our sodas, and peeled back wrappers. This would continue to be the dynamic of Dad's construction projects. There were always lots of kids ready to work for hours and all for a trip to the North Side grocery.

On the return trip it dawned on me that Dad hadn't punished and seemed extremely pleased. Obviously there was a purpose to this madness. With this thoughts of a whipping and tongue lashing fled my mind. Now I wondered more than anything what was he up to? That night as Dad sat the dining room table he started scribbling on a piece of paper. There was a simple drawing and a list of lumber and other items. This was when I was informed we were building a family room and adding a bathroom. Up to this point the four of us had struggled to share one bathroom.

Several years ago my father had taken on a project on the Spencer farm which at that time was located across the road from the Hillsboro airport. At the time I was only 4 years old with the role of spectator. The silo had several long heavy beams running from floor to ceiling and walls made up of tongue and groove 2x6 timbers. Dad carefully took down silo preserving each piece as if he had a plan. This was 2 years before me moved to the house on Forest street. Within a few short years to beautiful old farm house was raised and in its place a motel build.

We loaded these beams and boards of old growth timber onto the truck. They hung down the truck bed and were supported at the other end by the trailer. We then headed to the saw mill in North Plains where Dad had made arrangements to have the lumber milled lumber down to show its beauty. This removed the old silver color of the wood and exposed the beautiful golden color of the exposed grain.

We next needed to make room for a concrete slab. This would be the floor for the new family room. We shoveled out dirt by hand then loaded it on to the truck and trailer. Took it to the landfill and came back to do it again.

We then put in all the plumbing for the new bathroom and laid down the forms to create two long slabs each 8 feet wide and 20 feet long. We then hauled loads of gravel in and packed it down. We were now ready for the concrete.

The day the concrete started arriving in large trucks all the neighborhood kids turned out to help. The big trucks would back into our side yard with hardly room to spare between our house and the neighbors. Some kids in boots and others in sneakers walked through the concrete to spread it out over the slab. Dad took the job of smoothing the concrete as kids slopped through the concrete to finish filling the second slab.

The worked progressed with framing, wiring, windows, and insulation. Most of this was done by my brother, father and myself. The roof was made up of an exposed ceiling using the beams from the silo. The beautiful exposed beams running across the short length of the room and the boards that had made up the walls of the silo nailed up perpendicular to the beams.

The roofing was its own undertaking as Dad didn't want to pay for roofing shingles. So we started taking adventures into the Oregon coast range at the Tillamook burn. We searched for cedar snags, that is trees already dead of Western Red Cedar. We then cut the snag down and split it up into rounds. My brother and I would roll the sometimes giant rounds to the pickup and up into the bed. We had to pack in as many rounds as possible to satisfy Dad that we were doing a good job. We would then drive out on the dirt and gravel roads back to highway 26 and back to the house. We then unloaded the rounds hopped in the truck and headed back out to keep collecting cedar.

Using a mallet and a froe we would trim the sides of the rounds and then slice shingles from the rounds. Since cedar has a nice grain and likes to be split it was an easy job. The difficult part of the job was the number of shingles that were needed to cover the whole house. The froe is similar to a long knife but instead of the handle being in line with the knife its set at a 90 degree angle. This allowed you to start the shingle and one part way down the leverage of the handle allowed you to pop the shingle free.

Once we had a 4 foot cube of shingles we would bungle them together so that they were easier to move. We started the roof by covering it with roofing felt to improve the waterproofing. Then it was time to move the bundles of shingles to the roof. My brother and I huffed and puffed but they were just to heavy to carry up the ladder. Dad soon appeared at the edge of the roof wanting to know where the blazes his shingles were. He had to come down from the roof to make the determination himself but the shingle bundles were just too heavy.

We worked for a couple of weeks nailing shingles to not just the family room but to the remainder of the house. To finish it off Dad ran a copper wire along the top of each ridge to prevent moss from growing and prolong the roof life. Dad developed a side business with the shingles and we split shingles and roofed some of the neighbors homes.

The last thing constructed were shelves. The ones along the wall near the kitchen would be a pantry and another set for storage. Dad wanted doors to cover the shelves so he built the doors. They had beautiful louvers on the upper half that were quite tedious and difficult to make. I remember quite clearly the first door he made as the obscenities wafting from the garage became quite heated.

Eventually all the tasks were completed the family room was finished. We moved in furniture, then the TV ready to start enjoying the extra space. That winter despite all our hard work a leak developed in the roof. Dad determined the pitch and slope in the roof as it met the rest of the house caused water to collect. He implemented a temporary work around that saw us through the winter. The next spring we were back on the family room roof framing up a new roof line to eliminate the water problem.

CHAPTER 5

Building the Fireplace

The first home my parents purchased was on Forest Street in Hillsboro Oregon. We moved from the Hawthorne farms farm house rental witch would eventually be sold to Intel. They day we moved it rained and the new house was cold. I picked up the phone in the kitchen and there was someone talking. Not knowing what a party line was I thought there must be someone else in the house. It was an exciting day that Mom and Dad topped off by driving to Beaverton so that we could have pizza. Beaverton was the closest place to Hillsboro with pizza at the time.

The house was a 3 bedroom ranch home on a small city lot. You entered in through the living room with the kitchen on the left and a hallway leading straight back to three bedrooms and a single bathroom, to the left of the kitchen was a laundry room and garage. It was a big change from our small country house on Hawthorne farms where we had been surrounded by wheat fields. Here our nearest neighbor was 15 feet away instead of 1 mile. The house was built in 1958 the same year I was born making it 60 years old as of this writing. When we moved in it was 6 years old, the primary heating in the un-insulated house was forced air gas.

The furnace did the job but not to my father's satisfaction. He had grown up using fireplaces and woodstoves and knew how much more comfortable and inviting a home heated with wood could be. Once Dad decided he wanted to heat the home with wood, he and Mom made the decision to put a fireplace in our living room. There was no discussion as far as I know about who would be cutting and splitting firewood but I suspected that my brother and I would be nominees.

We would need materials and as my father grew up in the latter half of the depression saw no reason to purchase when it could be salvaged. The first bricks that Dad identified were on the Hillsboro sewer treatment plant property located South of town on first street adjacent to Jackson bottom.

The spring had been very wet and there had been flooding all over. When we got down near the old Carnation plant there were police and a road block. Highway 219 where it went through Jackson bottom was covered with water. There was no doubt to the water height as there was a fellow sitting on the roof of his Ford pickup as it floated in the water over the road. This was great entertainment at the time and we spent a significant part of the morning talking with the police and watching them float a small boat out the to the stranded motorist. The officer there was Sargent Poe, many years later after his death my father and Poe's widow would move into together to share a house.

Eventually the water went down and we were able to access the old brick building on the Jackson Bottom Slough, today this is called the wetlands preserve. Dad and I hitched up our utility trailer behind the old 1949 Chevrolet pickup and headed to the sewer treatment plant on Saturday. Dad backed the truck and trailer up to the old building, picked up his sledge hammer and walked into the building through the door. The old wooden roof was long gone.

Dad placed his hands against the front wall and without swinging the sledge brought the whole thing to the ground. Shortly after all four walls were lying on the ground. We then started the loading. The bricks were mostly still stuck together with mortar so we were moving large chunks onto the trailer and finally bringing the sledge to bare breaking down the largest chunks.

We pulled out the sewage treatment plant turning left and headed south on highway 219 towards the town of Scholls. About 5 miles down road we came to a 4 acre plot of land East of the road. Dad had purchased this property in hopes of building our first home on the location. The front two acres were pasture and the back two acres were much the same but included a few large douglas fir trees.

The property had a shallow well that Dad had hand dug and used a surface pump to the draw the water. This is also where Dad kept our old 1920's steel wheel tractor along with the plow and disk harrow and spike harrow. This tractor was my first exposure to using a hand crank to start a vehicle.

With an excessive amount of groaning, shoving and pushing the clumps of bricks were unloaded into a pile, we then climbed back into the truck and headed for home.

The next day armed with hammers, an old angle grinder and safety goggles and ear plugs we descended on the bricks. Mom, my brother and I chipped away at the mortar on the bricks while Dad used the angle grinder to smooth off each brick. Weekend after weekend we spent chipping at the 50 plus year old mortar. It was a satisfying feeling when a large chunk of mortar would fall away but was quickly be replaced by a grimace as small pieces of mortar stung your face. We spent several weekends chipping at the mortar then loading the bricks back into the pickup to be hauled back to the Forest street house and then unloaded once again.

During one trip Dad found a nest of mice, my brother and I played with the mice for a while and then decided to take them up to our tree house. The tree house was really only a platform of boards nailed to a tree 10 feet off the ground. We played with the mice and constantly herded them away from the edge of the platform so that they would not fall to the ground. At one point we had the mice all heareded together near the tree when as if on queue the mice exploded into there won great escape. They each headed in a separate direction almost as if they had planned the escape. We were 10 feet up the tree and just in time to see the mice reaching the ground and all running away, again each in a different direction. We descended the tree by the ladder to look for any injured mice but the escape had been clean and as far as I know none of the mice were ever captured.

This was the year between my first and second year. I had not done well in Mrs. Peach's class and thinking I might be having trouble seeing the black board she moved progressively closer to the front of the room as the year proceeded. When I reached the first row I still couldn't make out the black board so it was time to make a call to my parents.

Dad made an appointment with an optometrist in town named Alfred Furie. Doctor Furie would end up being a longtime friend who was understanding and had a deeper knowledge of acedemics then my parents.

Dr. Furie first sat me down at a device that was looking through a pair of binoculars. He then placed different cards in the device and asked me questions. This I would come to know tested my vision for color and depth perception among other things. He then took me a long room with a chair at one end and a funny device that I had to look through. Using this device with various lenses he was able to determine my vision requirements. Then with Dad's help I selected a pair of frames. This was the easiest step as Dad pointed at the cheapest pair of black plastic frames. The next week we went back to Dr. Furie where he took his time carefully fitting the new frames to my face and making sure they wouldn't fall off my face if I looked down.

With greatly improved vision I returned to the class room to finish the year, but the damage had been done and I would have to attend summer school to catch up with my class.

I started summer school at the same time we were cleaning bricks on the property. This wasn't to difficult as there were only a handful of students and I rapidly made up all of the class room work that I had failed. After class in the morning Dad would pick me up and we would go over to Hillsboro to do errands or on some days we would go to Artic Circle for a burger, fries with ice cream afterwards. For many years this was the main burger joint in town until in Burgerville USA opened in 1966. A few years later the McDonald's opened across the street from Burgerville.

My first pair of glass were doomed to only a short few months of life. One summer in the late afternoon my friend Donald and I were playing in his garden. He lived across the street where the house each sat on a half-acre lot. We had a hoe and shovel and dug vigorously in the dirt then would run Donald's toy trucks in and out to haul away the dirt. During a break we were talking about my new glass when Donald declared that they would break easy, not to be daunted I replied they were made of safety glass and could take a beating. This interplay continued for several minutes until I jumped up, tossed my glasses to the ground, then picked up the hoe and struck the glasses a vicious blow thinking I would show him. But it was not to be, the frame and the lenses both broke leaving me bug eyed with mouth hanging open. I picked up the pieces of my broken glasses and ran home.

That night Mom and Dad asked what had happened to my glasses, I showed them to the broken pieces and then told them the story. I must have mightily embarrassed as that is the only reason that I can think of that caused me to do what I did next, I told them how Donald grabbed my glasses and smashed them with a hoe. With this Dad went across the street to speak with Donald where as you might guess he got a different story. Well I'm a lousy liar and admitted that it was my fault and I was sorry. Then I had to apologize to Donald. Unfortunately this damaged our short relationship beyond all repair. A few months after this they moved away.

During all of this we were clean bricks every weekend and hauling them back to the Forest street house. Dad then hired a man to build the fireplace who had previous experience. Dad had some experience laying bricks but had very little idea how to build what he wanted.

The hired man arrived to start the work on a cool September day. He cut a huge hole in our living room wall and floor then built forms to create a footing for the fireplace. Into this footing went gravel and then mixed one wheel barrow at a time he filled it with concrete, this would be used to hold the weight of the bricks stacked above. He covered the hole with plastic that night. That was the last we ever saw of him. I remember Dad calling him several times, there was angry shouting but the fellow never came back.

Dad started by going to and old set of craftsman books he had picked up in a garage sale. He found plans for a fireplace suited his needs. This was many years before we had home improvement TV and Home Depot to help us out. We couldn't spend the winter with a plastic wall so Dad started building the fireplace. He found out an old set of brick layers tools and my brother and I stacked bricks in the side yard near the site. He started slowly mixing his first ever batch of mortar then laying the first course of bricks. He took care to make sure this first course was true and level. All the while his back side stuck out in the rain from under the plastic tarp. Fortunately Dad found some help from a local man who updated the design for best efficiency and lent a hand with some of the difficult portions. After this fireplace went up quickly and we had to make several trips to the property to haul more bricks to the job location.

Eventually Dad was ready to place the firebox, this is a heavy sheet metal enclosure with a vent at the top that could be adjusted for proper airflow. The hearth was raised up about 18 inches to make a place to sit and at the ends had vents to draw in cooler room air from low down in the room. Above the firebox was a vent that allowed even more heat to flow from the fire place.

The vent openings were covered over with Dad's own ingenious trick. He took bricks and sliced them in to pieces about ¾ of inch in width. Then then set them in mortar with space between them to finish the fireplace.

The fireplace came out wonderful and amazingly very efficient; a small fire would quickly heat the room and provide enough heat for much of the remainder of the house. I was proud of my father, it seemed there was nothing he couldn't build. As it turned out this was all good practice for laying concrete blocks in the basement foundation several years later. It was a pleasant Christmas that year with the hole filled in and the warm heat of the fireplace toasting our back sides.

After school we would come home and start a fire to heat the house. My brother and I would stand on the hearth to slowly turn and alternatingly bake each side. We were joined by our Siamese cats who would toast until they reached the peak of relaxation and slowly slither away to cool off. The only true down side was all the cords of wood we gathered and split over the years.

The following summer our cats found an additional use for the fireplace, one quite unintended. They were not outside cats, they were allowed outside under supervision occasionally and at other times would make a break for an opening door and escape. For the first time that summer we saw the cats on the roof of the house, I'm sure you have already figured out how they were able to climb pass the eves of the house on to the roof. After putting a ladder up and retrieving the wayward cat from the roof, we would search for but fail to find the means for the cats to access the roof. Mister Holt our neighbor and postman soon came to the rescue. He witnessed the cats climbing the fireplace and then the chimney, they would then work their way around to the roof side. They were really like little mountain climbers taking advantage of the gaps between bricks to reach the roof.

CHAPTER 6

Digging the Basement

My father grew up rough and tumble and he carried this over to us boys by being extremely strict. He believed corporal punishment was the punishment required for all transgressions and we saw a lot of it during our active boyhood. I can tell you there was no lasting harm and if anything they probably saved our lives. The belt educated us by teaching us to pause and ask ourselves, what will Dad's reaction be?

The first home my parents purchased was on Forest street in Hillsboro Oregon. A three bedroom ranch with wooden shingle siding, located on a small city lot in Northwest Hillsboro. Over the years Dad took on several construction projects to enlarge the house. I once ask him why we did so much, his response was to keep use boys busy and out of trouble.

Dad's latest expansion idea was a basement. We had already completed a family room and a bonus room over the garage. This was a 1000 square feet divided into two rooms. One room consuming a third of the space was a game room. The remaining two thirds was a shop for Dad. In Oregon very few people sport basements due to the wet climate. A significant amount of extra work must be done to make sure the basement is sealed against moisture. Additionally we spend several months of the year under cloud cover and what person would want to add another dark space.

During summer break one summer I wandered into our small back yard to find a 8 foot square hole at the back of the house. One side of the hole lined up with the foundation of the house. My first thought was to run away, the last time something like this happened we built a family room. I enjoyed the rest of my summer day thinking all along that it would probably be my last.

After work Dad was home and had my brother and I in the back yard using picks and shovel's to enlarge the hole. This was to be what we called the bulk head for the basement. The wide entrance would allow us to move in Dad's large shop tools. The digging was slow as the ground was hard and required breaking up with a pick before it could be shoveled.

We would fill up the pickup, take it to the land fill and have to shovel out the dirt again handling all that dirt twice. Soon the ever present neighborhood boys showed up with there shovels and the race was on. The digging and unloaded of the truck went quickly that day until we had the hole at 8 feet deep.

After the last load with all of us boys hanging off the back of the truck we stopped at North Side grocery where everyone as Dad's treat got a soda and treat. At this point the boys didn't realize that this was only the beginning of something much bigger.

Next we started digging out below the house foundation so that we could get at the dirt under the house. At this point we weren't required to dig except when Dad was home so to my relief we go to spend our summer in other activities. Day after day we dug eventually supporting the foundation with wooden timbers. The opening started to look like an old fashion gold mine.

During the early stages we would filled the back of the 1968 Chevy pickup using buckets and a wheel barrow then driving the truck a few blocks to a fellow that wanted clean fill dirt. We would then have to shovel the truck out. Recently I drove by this spot. These are the apartments across from the Fir Lawn Memorial Park sign. At that time it was a steep slope and not the nice level spot it is today.

The extra unloading was taking its toll. The dirt removal seemed to go slower and slower as we had further to haul. Eventually Dad located a small red dump trailer made from the back end of a pickup. It had a large gear on the front along with a drum. A cable pulled up the front of the bed and wound around the drum. This made it a simple matter of backing the trailer up then hand cranking up the bed to let most of the dirt slide free. Then a short jump forward in the pickup completed the job. This also meant that one person could empty the trailer and have it back ready to fill again.

The trailer wanted it ounce of blood and took it due to a failure on the part of the builder to include a ratchet that prevented the drum from unwinding the bed dropping down. As you turn the crank you had to keep your wits about you and be ready to jump out of the way, if your hand slipped off the handle it would whip back around and crack you in the back of the knuckles. If you were really slow it might wack you several times. Thankfully there were never any broken fingers or hands. Once it was done spinning the bed of the trailer had dropped and you had to start all over again cranking.

There was a Birdseye packaging near downtown Hillsboro and not to distant from our home. When we were digging the basement they had started to close down operations, eventually it would be demolished in 1980s to make way for the new Washington County Jail. Dad heard about the sale of equipment from a neighbor who worked there and was able to purchase a pair of conveyors. The conveyors were brought home to help remove the dirt from the hole. First he setup a conveyor on legs so that it would carry dirt up through the bulkhead and deposited it into the trailer. Dad used his welding skills to construct a large hopper at the bottom, this allowed us to toss the dirt into the hopper where the conveyer would carry it up and out of the basement.

The conveyor and the trailer meant that work proceeded much quicker. The hard labor meant we developed bigger muscles and callouses on our hands. It was the same from start to finish, first you use the pick to loosen the dirt and then use shovels to toss the dirt in the conveyor hopper. The work progresses slowly and by Christmas we had cleared the width of the house and a six foot section that led to the front of the house along the right hand side.

The section leading to the front of the house was so we could reach the plumbing for the bathroom and kitchen. To make more head room these would have to be moved. We took time out from digging to dig in the front yard. We created a 5 foot wide trench 9 feet deep from the street to the house foundation. This allowed us to lower the drain pipe from the house and locate it under the floor of the future basement. Dad laid in the new piping and prepared it to connect.

The next door neighbor was a plumber and a friend, Dad offered to pay him to do the hook up to the city sewer and water. The plumber deep down in the hole worked quickly to connect the sewer line, each time I heard rushing water he would come running back. When he finished filling the hole witch finally earned us our PHD's (Professional Hole Digger).

That Christmas was the first one that I spent in Vermont with my relatives and grandparents. We still had about 2/3 of the dirt to excavate from under the house but with the winter rains it was becoming a mess driving the truck and dump trailer over the yard. When we arrived in Vermont there was no snow, on the way to my grandparents we drove through Stowe Vermont witch is a big ski area and even they had no snow. That night there was lots of talk about the snow and it impact on the ski lodges. I fell asleep on Granma's couch that night dreaming of playing in the snow.

The next morning there was 4 feet of snow with giant drifts rising above the windows on the house. When I woke on the couch all I could see was snow out the window. My brother and I played in the snow that day with two of our young cousins. It was lots of fun but by the end of the second day we were winding down.

Then the snow mobiles started to arrive. It seemed like everyone had had a snow machine from new to old, fast to slow. We enjoyed running the snow mobiles all over Grampa's farm with some of our older cousin. We had lots of cousins; my father had 7 brothers and sisters as did my mother. That meant we had 14 Uncles and Aunts and lots of cousins.

The next day everyone showed up for a snow play day. I got outside late and by then all the snow machines were claimed and none left for me. It wasn't long until an uncle showed up with a beat up spray paint orange snow machine. He offered it to me and I took it but with serious doubts. Turned out to be a good choice, I could out run everyone as it was the machine used for racing. Later that day up on the hill my father go by and warned me to slow down as it looked like I was doing at least 80 mph.

Christmas day saw all my Aunts, Uncles and cousins coming to my Grandma's house. The main floor of the house was small at about 800 square feet and we had 40 people in attendance. The 7 foot high tree in the living room had presents piled so high that you could only see the Christmas star on top of the tree.

I had great fun that day and meant some of my cousins for the very first time. After Christmas we travelled around the area visiting relatives we had not seen on Christmas and in general having a great time. Nearly everywhere we went there was snow to play in or snow mobiles to ride.

The time in Vermont passed quickly, as we prepared to leave Vermont I felt my normal home sickness. Vermont always felt more like home then Oregon though 50 years later Oregon now feels like home. Soon we were jetting back to Oregon where the snow stayed year round on top of the mountains.

I had asked several of my Aunts and Uncles to visit Oregon and some have but most never did. Vermonters seemed to be firmly entrenched in the idea that we still use dirt roads, ride on wagons and horses. I always say they watch too much television.

When we entered the house on Forest street we sensed something was not quite as it should be. We could hear the sound of running water and it was not until we opened the old access hatch for under the house that we discovered several feet of water shining back from our flashlights. The water was already within feet of the floor. Our since of urgency sky rocketed as we made the trip to the back yard, where we uncovered the hole we had dug for access to the basement. Our fears we confirmed as we were confronted by water nearly as high as the house foundation, with a distinctly sewer-ish smell wafting up out of the hole that.

I don't know where he found it but Dad borrowed a trash pump that night and we started pumping water out of the basement. The level of the water dropped slowly down but soon we came to realize that it wasn't going down much further. Dad racked his brain until he remembered working on the house sewer drain before leaving for Vermont. He was fairly certain at this point that this had to be where the problem was generating all the water.

We devised a plan to fix the issue or as it turned out to plug the hole. My brother and I inflated two inner tubes and tied a board onto the top, this would be Dad's method of transportation. Then while my brother carved a crude paddle, Dad put on his heavy rubberized foul weather gear. Then with duct tape I tapped my father into the suit, around his ankles and wrists then neck and waist. (Another use for duct tape)

We lowered the raft into the questionable water, I noted at this point there was some pretty disgusting debris floating in the water. I wrinkled my nose, looked at Dad and thought how nice it was him and not me. Dad grinned and with a chuckle slid onto the raft. He ducked his head to clear the foundation and paddled across poop reservoir to the drain pipe.

Once near the drain pipe he stopped and looked the pipe over but saw nothing above. Then using his hand and arms used them to follow the pipe down along the pipe and into the murky water. Soon he turned around and paddle his way back to the basement entrance. He had discovered the drain pipe clean out was missing its cover and with all the rain we had been having it was backing up any pipe that didn't push back.

Finding a block of wood he carved a plug for the hole. No going to the store, it was Sunday evening and there was nothing open much less the hardware supply. Again he paddled his way back across to the drain pipe. He reached down as before but was unable to seat the plug. He slid from the raft bracing his feet on the bottom best he could and again tried to insert the plug. This time he realized it was to large and need to be trimmed to fit.

He trimmed the plug several times in attempt to fit the plug but to no avail. Soon we saw him take a deep breath and disappear below the water. When he came up he used his knife to carve the plug. After several trips up and down he had the plug firmly in place. He pulled himself on the raft and made his way back where brother and I waited with the garden hose to slosh off the filth. The job was done and the pump quickly emptied out the remainder of the water.

The next morning the water had receded and left a horrible nasty mess so we left it to dry out for a few days. When I did go down I found our tools and motorcycles covered in filth. I pulled everything out to the back yard and hosed them down. I cleared the motorcycle engines by removing the spark plugs and using the kick started to expel the water. With an oil change and fresh gas they started with only a few kicks.

After what we had started calling the great flood we started to digging again. Work progressed quickly, due to Dad's after school schedule, before he came home from work we were to fill the dump trailers and dump it twice. I was driving by then and becoming quite proficient in backing the truck in and dumping the loads with an occasional smack in the knuckles from the trailer. After the second load we cleaned up and usually helped Dad start dinner. After dinner it was dishes then homework and if we were really lucky television.

By this time we were getting out of tossing range for the conveyor hopper so we brought in the next conveyor. It was green with a white belt and had no legs. Dad took the most expedient route and hung each end from the rafters. One end was over the hopper and the other near where we worked the face. The ropes made it easy to lower the end, move to another location and suspend it in place. Now several people could be tossing dirt onto the conveyor along its length.

On weekends Dad was again paying the neighborhood kids with soda and candy so the loads went much faster. While he was gone they would pile up huge loads of dirt ready to quickly reload the trailer. I was always very busy running the truck back and forth. Once a month was Mom and Dad's pinochle party night, on these nights we quit early and were left to our own designs.

I remember the day we approached the back corner of the basement where we removed the last shovel full of dirt. Dad had the biggest grin on his face as he scooped up the last shovel full and dumped it on the conveyor.

The floors were even and smooth, the wall jutted up perpendicular and straight from the floor. We had also excavated for a few feet under the garage floor. We would build concrete steps that led up to the garage and provided an inside entrance. The railing in the garage protecting people from dropping into the stair well was from the First Interstate bank in Hillsboro that had closed.

With summer coming we hardly took a break before we were building forms for the footings that went along the walls. The footings supported the concrete block walls. Using an old cement mixer that Dad salvaged, repaired and added a motor, we made our own recipe for concrete from gravel, sand, cement and water.

My brother and I would quickly scoop rock and gravel into the mixer along with water, then add a coffee can full of cement. Dad would was give it a once over and we would dump it into the wheel barrow. Then down the board propped up in the back yard into the basement where Dad poured the concrete into the forms. We worked hard and it took a lot of mixing to complete the job.

After one particular hot day Dad pulled out a large sheet of black plastic. It had been used for many tasks over the years from covering loads to homemade tent. He spread it over the back yard at about 20 by 30 feet and then ran the hose onto it to create our own readymade slip and slide.

We slid away the afternoon with the excitement building as we had 3 and 4 people sliding at the same time.

Dad decided that mixing the concrete for the floor was too much work. So after laying the concrete forms for the floor and stairs he had the concrete delivered. We also installed a 50 gallon barrel in the floor to act as a sump to collect water seepage and pump it out of the basement.

The walls were concrete block we hauled into the basement two at a time. There were hundreds of them and very heavy at about 30 pounds each. Behind the walls we installed two levels of drainage pipe and hand shoveled gravel in to the remaining space. This was all about controlling water in the basement.

The space was split into one third for a game room with pool table and the other two thirds were Dad's new shop. Up to this time we used temporary posts to support the house. Dad picked up large steel I beams at the old Birds Eye plant. We would use these to support the house and eliminate the need for posts.

There was a lot of straining to get the beams into the basement due to the lack of space and the weight. Once in we started jacking up the ends using blocks and hydraulic jacks until the beam was at the correct height near the floor. Each beam stretched across from concrete block wall to concrete black wall. Once the beams were in place we had wide open spaces with no posts to get in our way.

The last thing we did was to build a permanent cover for the bulk head using heavy diamond plate steel sheets. That and a padlock secured the entry access.

Many years passed by, I went to college and married and my parents had moved to a different home. I saw an article in the Hillsboro Argus, they had found an illegal pot grow operation in the basement of the house I grew up in. The same article stated that the operator had been caught due to high electrical usage. It also stated the person running the operation had built the basement for just that purpose but they couldn't figure out how he had disposed of the dirt and moved all the construction materials with none of the neighbors knowing. We all had a good laugh knowing there was years of blood sweat and tears that went into building the basement.

CHAPTER 7

Building the bedroom

Our home on Forest Street was a typical ranch style built in 1958. Three bedrooms and one bath are located along a hallway that starts near dining room kitchen area. My parents occupied one room and on the opposite side of the hall my brother and I shared the corner bedroom. The third bedroom was given over to Mom's sewing room and the closet to Dad's hunting gear.

My brother and I shared a over under bunk bed with my brother on the bottom and me in the top of bunk. Not sure how I ended up on the top bunk but most likely my brother was placed in the lower bunk and therefore in a safer location.

One night I awoke with light from the hall streaming into our bedroom and my Mom standing over me. My mind told me that this was quite the accomplishment as my bed was about 5 and one half feet off the floor and Mom was near the same height. I also noticed that my mattress was exceedingly hard and uncomfortable. Turns out Mom had been thrust from a deep sleep by the sound of a giant boom that shook the floor of the house. It was the sound of my six year old body dropping from the upper bunk on to the braided rag carpet on the floor. Unhurt I returned to my bed and slept the night away.

My brother and I spent much of our time in our bedroom playing and fighting. My favorite game was a football game, you lined up your players and when the switch was turned on they would vibrate across the metal board. The fights over the next several years grew to such a volume that the upper bunk and myself were moved into the sewing room and my brother had our old room to his self.

The sewing room was crowded but not to bad when compared with the late night fights with my brother before the move. This was also the room where my Dad kept his cloth's, so I was much interrupted and didn't have much privacy.

It was at this time that I began to build plastic models of airplanes and one of the small shelves in the room was given over so that I might display them. My brother at the same time took to building models of cars and motorcycles, but he was much better then I. While I slaved for hour working to make parts fit and keeping the glue from staining he would quickly assemble a superior model.

In downtown Hillsboro there was a small but well stocked hobby shop. There was a broad selection of models along with glue and paint. They also kept a good supply of chemicals for chemistry sets, HO cars and electric cars. In the back room was a large race track. For a fee you could race your electric scale sized cars on the eight lane track. The Hillsboro Hobby Shop is still located in downtown Hillsboro and while the items for sale have changed over the years it still has the same look and feel with the airplanes hanging from the ceiling, a scale train model in the front window side by side with rockets.

It was about this time we saw a special on TV that talked about sightings of big root, also known as sasquatch. Most of the sightings at the time had been in the Pacific North West. The show reenacted several of the incidents and before the show reached the end I had left to read in my room. The tails recreated generated ferocious nightmares for weeks. I would wake up screaming and covered in sweat. We moved my bed away from the window and this helped a little bit but eventually Dad came up with a solution. Dad placed his old wooden radio near my bed and placed it on a very low volume. This kept me company and it wasn't long until I stopped having the nightmares.

I have spent a lot of time in the woods where the sightings were made, but have never seen sign or track of the beast. There are areas in the Cascade mountain range that leave the short hairs on your neck standing on end. In these areas you will feel as though your being watched witch will cause your pulse to race and you will quicken your pace to leave the area. This also could be caused by the frequency of mountain lions in the area.

Eventually Dad decided after some discussion with the rest of the family that we should build a large bedroom for my brother and I. Dad was quite good with his hands and mastered many construction skills. He had a couple of basic rules. You should always overbuild, that is if the code required 2x6 beams twenty four inches apart he would use 2x8 beams 18 inches apart. The other rule was "there is no such thing as to many nails and other fasteners.

I came across Dad at the kitchen table one day drawing a sketch and making a list. This was his plan for building a bedroom above the garage which was at the front corner of the house and away from all the other bedrooms. If we were going to fight he wanted us far away from his bedroom so he could sleep. He worked graveyard shifts as a machinist at the time which meant he usually slept during the day time when we were in school.

Dad was ready to head to lumber yard so we piled in to his old Chevrolet pickup to accompany him. When we arrived at the lumber store we went into the office where Dad started discussing his needs with the estimator. I grew bored with this after a while and wondered out the back door and into the lumber yard. While walking along the mezzanine, an elevated walkway with a wooden railing, I drug my hand lazily along the railing looking at the stock of moldings. Soon I caught big splinter in my right hand just below my second finger. I pulled the large chunk of wood out of my hand then fishing around in my pocket for my folding knife I took to prying out several splinters that had been left behind.

When we arrived home I doused the wound with mercurochrome to prevent infection and it soon healed. In our house we had three cure-all solutions, mercurochrome and antiseptic powder to prevent wound infection. For everything else there was Bag Balm, this salve was originally developed to sooth cows' udders then eventually for irritated or chapped hands. As a young father I found Bag Balm a miracle cure for diaper rash. Unknown to me at the time there was still a splinter left in the wound, this would come back to haunt me.

On Friday Dad, my brother and I were on the roof of the garage removing shingles and tossing them off the edge of the roof. We continued working even when it started to become dark and Dad stung up some lights to illuminate the area. Everything was fine with me up to this point until it started drizzle rain. I looked towards the edge of the roof to see that it had become a drop in to a dark abyss. A little later I slipped on the roof sheathing; at this point I became frightened and found it difficult to move about. I would occasionally slip and then look towards the dark abyss. Dad came to my rescue by calling it a night. But then my anxiety escalated as I realized I would have to work my way down the roof edge where the ladder was located. I slowly and cautiously made my way down the roof on hands and knees until I reached the ladder. Here I had to lower myself on to the metal rungs that had become slippery with the moisture. I clung to the ladder with a fierce grip as I made my way down, sure that I would plummet to the ground at any time. Up to this point I had never really feared heights, respected yet but feared never. That night I gained a new respect for heights and the sudden stop at the end of a fall. This has since plagued me my entire life.

The next morning we started removing the sheathing from the roof witch exposed the rafters and the back side of the sheet rock that lined the roof of the garage. We removed all the standing members of the roof witch were not the prebuilt truss you see today, but hand made on site. We were left with a view of the back side of the garage ceiling.

The next day was Sunday. I awoke in bed unable to bend my right leg without excruciating pain. Once bent it would be fine until I tried to change position again. We went for a long drive in the car that day, I was in pain for most of the trip and unable to get out of the car when we stopped for breaks. When we got home with lots of help I was able with great pain to leverage up out of the car and make it to the living room couch. The next morning my knee still hurt but much less, so Mom kept me home from school, but by Tuesday I was back in class. I had several of these incidents over the years until finally at 30 years old the umpteenth doctor saw me and quickly diagnosed gout. People who suffer from gout are unable to eliminate the buildup of naturally occurring uric acid. The excess uric acid then forms crystals in your joints and tendons.

The following weekend we were up and back to work on the new bedrooms. Dad rousted us out of bed just as the sun was coming up. After breakfast we quickly dressed for the cool weather. I wore my green jeans, not blue jeans. Dad felt that James Dean and his iconic blue jeans were a bad influence and wouldn't let us wear blue jeans even though half the kids at school wore them. I also put on my heavy green sweat shirt. With my leather gloves and hammer I found myself the first one to arrive on the garage roof. I started to walk across the edges of the slippery beams my only thought was that Dad would be proud of my initiative. It was at this point my front foot slipped from the beam and I found myself astraddle the beam and in great pain down near the nether regions. This must have been what someone meant when they said "Pride goes before the fall". My father arrived and his first question was why did I ruin his garage ceiling. I didn't really care at this point as I was still in some pain. I saw my brother at the top of the ladder drop back down only to return as my father was pulling me out of the holes I had left. Apparently his quick departure was so that he could see what my legs looked like dangling in the garage and what a terrible mess I had made. Dad didn't seem overly wrought and we continued with our daily labor which now included cutting new sheet rock to repair the holes.

Next came the flooring. As we nailed down sheets of 5/8 inch plywood my brother commented I would no longer be able to enter the attic using the garage ceiling. Putting the flooring down made it much easier and I felt less anxiety then when I had stood on the roof.

Next we started building the framing. The bedroom would be one large room with a window at either end. One looking out over the street would be my brothers end and the one looking out the back mine. We had one long closet with sliding doors that we shared and at my end I had a hidden door that led into the attic that was over the first floor of the house.

Throughout the construction we hauled each piece up to the roof by hand. It was an arduous task but our young bodies recovered quickly after a hard days work. When it came time for the roof Dad took pity on us all and had trusses constructed and delivered. This allowed us to put up the roof structure, sheath the roof and shingle all in one weekend. I couldn't manage getting on the roof out of fear so Dad's friend Bill helped out.

Next was the siding. Dad enlisted his friend Bill again to help, they would each climb a ladder and us boys would hand them up the sheet. They then hoisted the sheet into place and nailed it in place. In the yard we setup several saw horses. We would drop a piece of siding on the horses, pour a liberal dosage of paint on the sheet and then race to see who would finish painting there half. By the time we finished siding the bedroom each of us liberally covered with paint. The siding was done and the room proof against the weather.

Dad stood us in the back yard where with liberal does of cold water from the hose we scrubbed at the paint. He had us remove our clothes and continue scrubbing in our skivvies. We next moved to the bathroom tub where we used abrasive lava soap and scrub brushes to remove the remainder of the paint and several layers of hide.

The stairs to the second floor bedroom were constructed almost exclusively by Dad. They were made of wood and painted grey. The top end let out into my brothers side of the bedroom which would eventually cause several conflicts.

By the time school let out for the summer the new bedroom had stairs but no electricity or insulation. I asked permission and was granted to start sleeping up stairs. I setup a crate with a lamp so that I could read and an old army cot. The lamp was plugged into and extension cord that went down the stairs and into the laundry room. This turned out to have a great advantage, while it was terrible hot during the day it cooled off quickly at night.

While working on the electrical outlets in the bedroom Dad noted that I favored my right hand. It had developed a large knot over the old splinter wound and any pressure on it caused extreme pain. Dad didn't believe in unnecessary doctor trips but he allowed this didn't appear to be something for Bag Balm.

I soon found myself in the Chevrolet pickup truck headed for Doctor Nautical's office. The waiting room was nearly empty and without an appointment we were soon seen by the doctor. After the exam we joined the doctor in his office where he lit a cigarette and told Dad he had determined I had a nerve bundle formed over the old splinter and that it require surgery to remove. Dad made an appointment for the next week.

When we arrived at the Doctor Nautical's office Dad took off to run errands in town I was ushered into a room I had never entered. In the surgery room I was made to lie on the table and then stretched my arm on to some supports with my palm pointed at the ceiling. The doctor came in and let me know we had a great opportunity. He had a couple of interns from the hospital that day that would be interested in observing the surgery. He asked my permission and I thought a couple more future doctors, no problem.

The door opened and Doctor Nautical escorted in five interns, three men and two woman. Having watched doctor shows on TV I knew the next thing they would do was to anesthetize me. I was all in for a surgery where I didn't have to witness the process. I waited to be anesthetized but instead an injection to numb my lower arm was give. I was to be conscious during the procedure. The room was darkened except for the surgery lights and the doctor started in explaining each step. I was able to avert my eyes but couldn't close my ears as he went into gruesome details for the benefits of the interns. This was really too much for me, I turned my head firmly to the left to avoid watching. The interns were fascinated with the process and encouraged me to observe the process. Through-out the surgery they encouraged me to look and described the details. It was at this point that I wanted to say no interns. The surgery was a success and my hand healed quickly with no further pain.

We finished the interior walls with insulation and inexpensive simulated wall paneling. Dad also built two sets of shelves for books, models and knickknacks. We moved in and enjoyed the large space. On rainy days there was enough room to have several friends over to play games and have wrestling competitions.

Dad brought home a 20 foot long rope that would stretch and stretch when you pulled on it building up pent energy until it was released. My brother and I took the rope to the side yard and each took and end, we wanted to see how far it would stretch. We each took an end, then the pulling started. We pulled and pulled stretching it out farther and farther, then bracing our legs to pull some more. Then I heard my brother snort and then bray with laughter as he let his end of the rope go. There was scarcely time for me to release my end of the rope but all to late it plowed into me like a bus driver meeting a schedule. The pain was intense as the rope struck my thighs, stomach, chest and especially my boy regions. I fell to the ground holding my groin and moaning in pain while my brother laughed all the harder. On another day I got out the rope bent on revenge but again my brother was the quicker and let go of his end first. I was expecting it this time and only suffered minor damage. After that I made the rope disappear.

Eventually we reached a point where we wanted our own rooms. Dad build a wall down the center splitting the large room and giving us each our own space.

Returning from a Boy Scout back packing trip we found new carpet in our bedrooms. Mom had laid alternating one foot stick on carpet using neon red and blue. We liked it instantly but some of our friends found it difficult to traverse especially as on sunny days the carpet could be dazzling.

Through our shared closet space was a man sized hole with a cover that let into part of the attic. Immediately inside this opening was the kitchen stove vent that emptied into the attic. My brother found that but sitting quietly with the access open you could hear conversations in the kitchen. I tried it out but found I didn't have the patience to sit around until something interesting was said.

We really enjoyed our bedrooms; I used mine until I was 21 and left to go to college at Oregon State University. While in college Mom and Dad built a new nicer home four blocks away.

CHAPTER 8

Flying the coup

I grew up in rural Washington County living on a street of homes, each with its own small lot. The first pets we had were fish, guppies to be more specific. The fish were a test to see if we qualified for more difficult to care for pets. The guppies came pregnant so that within a few days we had gone from two to 20 fish. This success meant that we could move on to the next challenge of raising kittens.

Our first cats ended up being two Siamese cats. Why two cats you might ask? Because my brother and I each wanted our own cat and didn't want to share. My cat was a blue point Siamese I named Missy while my brother chose a dark seal point Siamese kitten he named Candy. Both kittens grew to be very fun and cuddly. There was one down side we had not expected, Siamese cats are very vocal. They cry for their food, they cry when they can't find you.

It's not possible to accidently lock a Siamese cat in a closet or bedroom as they with sound off like a fire truck.

Candy grew up loving each of the family members and a handful close friends. All others were not welcome. She took to hanging out on top of the refrigerator; this was located at the end of the hall way coming from our bedrooms. If you were someone she didn't know or like, out would come the paw to bat you going by.

Even with these aggressive behaviors she tolerated some strangers but kept one rule very strict, no touching the tail. Retribution was swift and sure. At one time my friend Kenny went racing up the bedroom stairs and quite by accident stepped on the tip of her tail. Kenny was in stocking feet and she did not cry out so we thought no harm no foul. An hour later Kenny headed down the stairs to use the facilities and Candy laid in wait around the corner. She pounced on his legs and with a awful howl and hiss dug in and attempted to lay waste to his leg. Fortunately he was wearing tough blue jeans and was able to kick free. I had never seen Candy act that way and it was to be the only time we knew of it occurring.

Candy was also a food thief and would use clever ploys to distract you and then make the snatch and run. One method left my father bent out of shape. He couldn't put down a can of beer or leave it for a moment for quick as you please she would grip the can and slurp the beer up through the opening without knocking the can over.

For Thanksgiving Mom search the markets for a large turkey. We were to have family over and that meant lots of food was needed. That year two of my father's brothers and there families were coming to our house. She braved the wild streets of Hillsboro, and then broadened her search to Cornelius. At long last she found the prey she sought. His name was Tom and he was all of 20 pounds. Mom smiled to herself as she carried Tom in her grocery cart to the check-out stand.

There was a problem with Tom, he was frozen straight through and due to the time needed to find him there was little time left to thaw him out before the big day. Upon arriving home the kitchen sink was scrubbed and sanitized. Then Tom still in his plastic shirt was left to defrost overnight.

That night we gathered around the TV and enjoyed a simple sit-com. Candy sat in my brother's lap contented and purring. Missy slowly worked her way from my lap to under my chin. She was very affectionate and easily demonstrated it. At bed time she would curl up on top of my covers happy to be nearby and tolerant of my tossing and turning. She occasionally would check on my and look for a pet and reassurance, I would then wrap my arms around her and fall asleep to her purr. In my brothers room candy would curl up under the covers and sleep most of the night.

I had nodded off to sleep with my light on and a new paperback firmly grasped in my hands. I startled awake but with no remembrance of what woke me. I listened and heard a gentle thump, a shock ran through me and I remembered last year's Christmas incident when my brother and I had thought someone was trying to break into the house.

My nerve started to string tight and I perked my ears to listen harder if that's possible and heard a double thump and thump. Again it was the same quiet sound. I thought about pulling the covers over my head but other than the thump the house was quiet witch might mean no one else was up.

I arose and slid into my robe and slippers, opened my closest door and pulled out my baseball bat. I then crept to the stop of the stairs continuing to strain my ears. I quietly moved down the stairs, this was no mean feat as they were all wood and while new squeaked on occasion.

I stepped down the long length of the laundry room. The banging was louder as I opened the door to the kitchen. The noise coming from the kitchen window to my right but my view was blocked by the refrigerator.

Quite unexpectedly there was the sound of an enormous weight falling to the floor. I jumped and turned to run from the kitchen but instead flipped on the lights to the kitchen. I saw my mother in her robe standing in the hallway to the down stairs bedrooms. Mom exclaimed "What in the world is going on?"

Mom and I both turned towards the kitchen sink. Have you guessed yet? Candy, all 7 pounds of her had drug 20 pound Tom from his resting place in the sink onto the floor, where growling and tugging she attempted to drag off her victim by the netting surrounding him.

Mom rescued the Tom then turned her wrath upon Candy. Candy stared at Mom with an innocent look and then slowly turned to look at me. Mom slowly turned and vented her wrath upon me asking what I was doing out of bed. I held my tongue but wanted to say isn't obvious Candy woke me up.

Eventually I returned to my bed where I found my kitty Missy keeping it warm. I fell asleep with a grin on my face thinking of that little cat and the turkey.

The next day was Thanksgiving. When I awoke I smelled turkey, Mmmm wonderful turkey. Mom and Dad were preparing the feast in the kitchen. I opened my mouth to speak but hesitated, where had Mom gotten the turkey? There were no stores open again until the day after Thanks giving. Mom turned and saw me, winked and said "doesn't that turkey smell wonderful".

I let my mouth close. I dared not speak but questions have haunted ever afterwards.

CHAPTER 9

Christmas and the crazy old man

As a child did you ever awaken Christmas morning, creep down the stairs to the family tree to see if Santa had arrived? For my brother and I this was our yearly ritual. There were set rules for Christmas morning, we could only open our stockings, no presents; we were not to awaken Mom and Dad.

Most years my brother and I did just what we were supposed to do. Accompanied by our cats Missy and Candy we played with the small toys from the stockings and stayed quiet. We might even risk turning on the Christmas tree lights.

Our two wonderful Siamese cats named Missy and Candy were always present for exciting events. You might have read about Candy in "Candy and the turkey". Siamese cats are very vocal. There is no hesitation in voicing displeasure with circumstances. I once shut the cat in the bedroom and she left no doubt as to her location and level of unhappiness. Our current cat Abby is so quiet, if she is caught behind a door we have to instigate a search to find her.

Christmas that year was wonderful. We rarely have snow on the ground during the holidays this year it had snowed two days earlier and two inches of the white wet stuff remained on the ground. The Christmas tree was up, the real thing, a 6 foot Douglas fir from the forests of Oregon cut by us boys from a local farm. Not a tree farm, but friends who owned a wood lot on a local farm let us cut a tree. The tree stood next to the used brick fireplace that my father constructed.

We hung our tree from a swag hook in the ceiling as the cats frequently climbed the tree witch in turned caused the tree to topple and ornaments to break.

My mother then president of the local Legal Secretary organization prepared for the bazar. She found wooden ornaments that came unpainted and punched out of thin sheets of wood. My brother and I separated the parts, sanded, glued and painted each one under Candy's watchful eye. When we had completed the ornaments we would be presented with more sets to be completed. They sold-out at the bazar each year which was great for the Legal Secretaries and kept us boys busy for several weeks.

As the day of Christmas approached my brother and I became more and more excited. Christmas vacation was quickly approaching witch meant no school for more than a week. The snow that came two days before Christmas caused even greater excitement. Then Mom started baking Christmas cookies. We would take large plates of cookies to the neighbors who in turn would bring us treats. Mrs. Holt across the street always brought her fruit cake witch was quite delicious.

Christmas eve found us in our bedrooms upstairs. We were too excited to sleep but thanks to my father's foresight at placing us upstairs and across the length the house we did not disturb Mom and Dad's sleep. Eventually we drifted off to sleep with dreams of what lay ahead, our respective joining us. Candy tucked under the covers of my brothers bed and Missy sprawled across the covers on top of me.

The next thing I knew was whispering. My brother was hanging over me whispering, "wake up, wake up its Christmas". It was very early, I looked at my clock, 3 AM. Missy was curled up between my legs peacefully asleep. I slowly pulled my legs up and around Missy who was still enthroned upon the bed. She was one affectionate cat and would soon join me.

The room was cold and I quickly dressed. The rest of the house would be at least as cold and we wouldn't dare turn on the heat or start a fire in the fireplace for fear of waking Mom and Dad. We made our way down the stairs and passed the dark window in the laundry room, then across the kitchen to the living room. As we went our speed increased until we came to a sliding stop in the living room.

Our stockings sat on the fireplace hearth bulging with presents and brightly wrapped presents were piled under the tree. If possible our excitement grew. Missy crossed the kitchen and sat on the living room floor carefully cleaning her paws. We crossed to the fireplace to open our stockings. Missy joined us and at sat at my feet, calm and collected.

We had small tops, and electronic toy to assemble, a bag of candy and tangerines. Moments later brother and I were munching on candy and petting Missy by the light of a single lamp. The house still cold and dark. I peaked out the window but only saw my reflection and the distant street light. I shuttered with the cold, my brother was looking at me strangely his eyes slightly bulging. "What was that"! I now listened and heard what he already had noted, a quiet strained voice saying "help me". This was repeated several times along with a soft rap at on the front door. Shivers traveled up and down my spine. Who would be at our door so early Christmas morning?

My brother disappeared in to the kitchen where he pulled himself onto the counter to look out the front window. I joined him but all we saw was the dim darkness softly lit by the distant street light. We then moved back to the living room and peered around the front curtains out into the dark again. There was no way we could see the front steps.

The soft tapping returned along the repeated cry of help me. We crouched lower, now in terror, I grabbed the blanket off the back of the couch and we sat hidden underneath. "Bro" I said, "we need to get Dad!" This was a new terror, disturbing Dad might invoke the second coming and our final demise. "No, no" said my brother our fear of Dad almost as great.

The noise from the front door continued and with every moment we knew we had to do something. Stepping close together we moved to the front door and steeled ourselves to open the door but we could not do it so overcome with fear.

We knew something had to be done. There was a sense of urgency, my brother finally said he would wake Dad. He crept quietly down the hallway to the master bedroom and repeated the same with Dad as he had done with me that morning. I stood behind him as he whispered "Dad, we need you". Dad snorted quietly and his eyes opened, with more intensity my brother said "Dad there's a crazy man trying to break into the house"! Dad's eyes shot open but he didn't move. "Crazy man at the door" he said. "Did you look to see who was there?"

I responded with a shake of my head but realized he couldn't see me, "No" I replied. He then asked if we had turned on the porch light? Again the answer was no. Dad turned and picked up the clock bringing it close to his myopic eyes and said "Boys, did you know its 4 AM?"

Dad fumbled with his glasses and being careful to not wake Mom rose from the bed and drew on his robe. We then head towards the front door with Dad in the lead. It may have been my imagination but he appeared to be moving slow and quiet, similar to how we would hunt together.

Reaching the door, Dad grasped the knob and leaned his ear against the surface of the door. We could still hear the voice call out, this time the cry was indiscernible but the soft knock that followed was the same. I looked around for Missy. Our cats were indoor only creatures but never passed up an opportunity to escape and possible make it into the street. No Missy, so we wouldn't have to worry about her escaping.

Dad switched on the front porch light, the noise stopped, he opened the door. Now nothing separated us from the crazy man except the flimsy screen. I wanted to scream at Dad, "watch out" but remained quiet. He opened the screen door and with a chuckle let my brothers cat Candy in to the house. "Poor Candy" my father said, "mean boys wouldn't let you in". I breathed with a sigh of relief.

We dried Candy then set her on the fireplace hearth to warm before the fire that Dad had started. She basked in the attention and warmth. Mom was awake by now and joined us in the living room. Missy came back from wherever she had wandered. Since everyone was awake we opened our presents. In a few hours the relatives would arrive but for now Missy crouched under the wrapping paper and batted at bows, Candy lay sprawled before the fire absorbing the heat.

The meal was being prepared and we were all dressed in our best as our uncles, aunts and cousins arrived. As each one arrived Dad related the story of the crazy old man. "Those boys woke me up at 3 AM because they were afraid to a let a little cat into the house." Everyone laughed and wanted to hear more, witch we related to them.

I was relieved that Candy was ok but though we racked our brains we could never figure out when or how she had escaped the house. This was further complicated in that my brother had not noticed her absence at bed time, though this could be explained away with our before Christmas jitters. That night each of made sure that both Missy and Candy were in the house at bed time. That night Candy crawled under the covers and sighed with relief at the warmth and happily snoozed away the night.

CHAPTER 10

Tree house, Crawdads, Creek and Ghost

There were two brothers Daryl and Mack Buldony. Mack was older than me by a couple of years and Daryl was older than Mack. They were what we called real hell raisers, but they were part of the neighborhood group which was comprised mostly of boys. The boys in the neighborhood got together for all sorts of games and work. These boys were also involved with my father's projects; building a family room and digging a basement. There was at any time one girl in the general age category of the boys, the first was Deanna who was my age and rarely wanted to play. After Deanna moved, Lois and her two brothers moved into the house. Unlike Deanna Lois and her two brothers were always involved in our neighborhood activities.

The Buldony's lived at the end of the dead end. Their parents had three acres that we used to create a baseball field complete with back chicken wire back stop. We used what balls and bats we could come up with but the lucky ones had gloves. There was also a tether ball and pole vault. The pole vault lacked the landing pad but had a nice smooth landing zone of dirt. We took turns going higher and higher and amazingly there were no broken bones but plenty of bumps and bruises.

Across the street from from the Buldoney was a cherry orchard. We would at times slip in for a handful, but as they were very tall this meant shinning up the trunk then hanging off a branch for a handful of black cherries. On one occasion while in the orchard, four of us including Mack were spread out in the looking for low hanging fruit. Mack in his overalls with no shirt started kicking the trees in frustration, the rest of us were glad he decided to take his angst out against the trees. Soon the air was filled blood curdling screams. Mack went by at full speed screaming his fool head off. So the rest of us high tailed out of the orchard knowing something wasn't right. What had gone wrong was a swarm of hornets that Mack had stirred up. Seeing the bee I froze and didn't move a muscle therefore saving myself from a sting.

Eventually as the other boys disappeared out to toward the dead end I walked out of the orchard still looking for more bees. The boys were standing at a distance watching Mack dance his fool head off, with the screaming as accompaniment. He was screaming "get them out, get them out". The bees were apparently inside Mack's coveralls. My brother with his quick wit figured out that we could kill the bees by throwing dirt clods and rocks at Mack, hey no one wanted to get near a bee. Mack screamed even louder threatening revenge then went back to slapping his coveralls and screaming. Mack suddenly made a decisions and abandoned his coveralls, as he did several bees flew free from there imprisonment.

The summer before I had been stung so many times the doctor said I was having moderate allergic reactions. A sting in my foot would swell up until it reached my knee. I eventually stopped going barefoot but then when I was on a walk a bee flew from above and stung me in the eyelid. I was even wearing my glasses and it happen so fast I could hardly respond. That hurt something awful and put me out of action for a week. I became more and more paranoid and wouldn't wear shorts or tee shirts just jeans and long sleeve shirts. I also took to wearing a billed baseball cap.

I eventually I learned to stay calm around bees and to be aware of their buzzing. Needless to say I was relieved many years later when Sting Kill hit the market. Those little green vials were a miracle drug after all the stings I had survived.

Near the creek one summer Daryl Buldony started a tree house in a small group of Douglas fir at the bottom of an abandoned orchard. We didn't have permission to be on the property but just moved in as if we were the owners. We hauled boards from back yards and remnants from construction sites on the front handle bars of our bikes. With the board precariously balanced on the handle bars with one arm wrapped around the board and one hand on the steering wheel we would traverse the country road then down through the orchard. There were a few crack ups but since it was in a good cause there were no complaints

Daryl had started the first story of the tree house 12 feet off the ground by bolting together two 2x8 boards 10 feet long. Most of the work in the tree was done by Daryl at first as there wasn't much room for anyone else. The work progressed until there was platform in the tree 10 feet on each side. Daryl wouldn't let any of us do anything but poke are heads through the access hole to peak around. From this point on we spent our time handing boards up to Daryl so that he could put up a wall and then a flat top roof. Next he started on the second story by cutting a hole in the roof and again building walls and another roof.

Daryl would let us come up sometimes but he let us know it was his. Eventually he let us up to the first story but only when he was there. He enforced this by putting a door on the entrance in the floor and adding a padlock.

Since we weren't welcome we decided to build a fort at the foot of the tree. Since we weren't welcome Daryl was left to haul the boards up the tree on his own. We started by building a wall that surrounded half the tree and left the ladder to the tree house outside. It wasn't very pretty but everyone was welcome to help out and come inside.

We would bring our sleeping bags along some days and stay the night building a fire to roast our hot dogs and marshmallows. When it was good and truly dark we would sit around and tell ghost stories. This was usually all in good fun until one night Daryl told a story. That was one creepy story, the dark immediately seemed blacker and for the first time we noticed the wind moaning as it blew through the trees. With everyone staring back and forth and with very few words of agreement, we had grabbed our gear and headed out for the nearest home where we spent the night on the garage floor and feeling much safer.

Dairy Creek runs just a short walk from where the tree house resided. This is a small sluggish stream that crosses through the farms Northwest of Hillsboro. The creek has been renamed and can be found on maps as McKay creek. On hot days we would go down to the creek to cool off on the shaded banks. The water was shallow during the summer barely reaching knee height during the summer.

The creek is also full of crawdads. These look like miniature lobsters. While there claws are much small they can snap quite firmly and once hooked to nose, finger or toe are extremely difficult to remove. After a day at the creek we would return home and start planning what needed to be done on the tree house. There was a lot of arguing and less discussion but Mack would usually end it by threatening to smash our faces.

I have put a pleasant bent on this story but Mack and Daryl were big time neighborhood bullies. They cowed almost everyone and at one time or another they beat up each one of us. One summer day when I passed there house they called me into there driveway. Believe me you didn't want to run away and have them hunt you down. They were giving a hot time and I was sure a beating would ensue when there mother came out. She was a small woman nearly a foot shorter than either of her boys. I could tell she was angry as she waved her boys over and waved at them to bend down. Quick as you please she snagged the ear of each boy and headed for the house. Mack and Daryl screamed and squealed all the way into the house.

Most summer evenings we would play a game we made up and had named ghost. Many times since my childhood I have taught this game to groups of kids who also enjoyed playing it as much or more then we did.

How to play

You can play it almost anywhere that provides cover to hide but someone's home with a large back yard is best. You can successfully play it with as few as four kids and I have seen it played with more then 20. It should be played in the evening at dusk or in the dark as it makes it easier to hide.

One person is selected or volunteered to be the ghost. The ghost goes into the back yard and hides. Only one side of the house is fair to use, the other side is out of bounds and means your automatically the new ghost.

The others playing wait at base, usually the front porch or steps and counts to 100. Then everyone works their way through the side yard hunting for the ghost. Once the ghost is spotted, you shout "ghost" and everyone runs for base. Everyone touched by the ghost joins the first ghost. The next turn the ghost and all new ghosts join together and hide in the back yard again. This continues until one person is left. The person left becomes the new ghost and you start over.

We had fantastic fun and it got us out of the house. I remember someone hiding so well that we were at the back of the yard before they were spotted in the side yard. She nailed a bunch of us that time.

We continued to work on the tree house and club house eventually building a platform in a second tree and connecting it to the bottom level of the first tree house. The bridge was wide and easy to cross though most of us crossed it on hands and knees in trepidation of the quick stop at the bottom of the fall.

Near the end of summer the tree house adventure ended. A developer purchased the land for homes and informed our parents that we would need to remove the buildings. One cool fall day after school started we all showed up along with our fathers and there trucks. We worked together and quickly brought down all of our hard work. Coming down much faster than it went up. I was sad to see it go, it seemed an end to an era. It had also brought many of us much closer together and common good time memories.

CHAPTER 11

Separate bedrooms

My brother and I shared a bedroom when we lived on Hawthorne farms in Hillsboro Oregon, he in his crib and I in my bed. It was there we experienced the largest storm to hit the Portland Oregon area in a century, the Columbus Day storm. But this story is about sharing a bedroom and I will leave the story of the storm for another tale.

The first indication that sharing might lead to problems occurred in this room. My two year old brother wanted out of the crib, when Mom arrived I had him by the head, witch was sticking between the bars and with much twisting and turning attempting to free him.

The next event in this same room occurred one year later. I awoke one night to my brother screaming and my parents out of bed. I snuck to the hallway and down to where it joined the kitchen. From here I heard my brother excitedly explain that he had seen a lion in the kitchen. Mom and Dad sounded doubtful but in order to get sleep that night took him back to their bedroom. I slid back between the sheets to enjoy having the bedroom all to myself.

The next day Mom talked about the lion in the kitchen. My brother confessed that it might have been a shadow, but it really looked like a lion. The next night my brother awoke me and we crept into the kitchen. He suddenly stopped and his whole body shook as he slowly raised his arm and pointed. What I saw was the beacon light from the Hillsboro airport creating shadows on the wall. With a bit of apprehension I walked to the window and looked at the front yard in the dim light there were shadows, nut no lion anywhere.

Between kindergarten and first grade we moved into Hillsboro three blocks from Peter Boscow school. The home had three bedrooms, one for Mom and Dad, one for Mom's sewing room and one that I shared with my brother. It was different living there from the country where we had lived before. Our neighbors were close together compared to living on the farm where the closest neighbor was a quarter mile away.

My brother and I had bunk beds, I on the top and he on the bottom. The selection for bunk was made by Mom who stated she didn't want her baby so high in the air where he might fall. But on the otherhand it was apparently fine if I fell from the top. There was a low short rail near my head that was suppose to prevent me from falling but there were many nights when I woke up on the floor wondering how I had arrived.

The bunk arrangement lead to violent battles. Brother would become angry at me through my mattress from down below, then when I climbed down the ladder to administer my own form of punishment until the bedroom door would fly open with a mighty boom and Dad would be there to deal out his reprimand.

Our endless fights and battles disrupted the house hold and frequently prevented Mom and Dad from sleeping at night. I was happy to sleep through the night but was awoken by violent kicks from my brother. Eventually this would lead to the event that would top all those that had gone before.

Mom and Dad had monthly pinochle parties for years, each member taking turns hosting the event in their home. One fall evening the party was in my parent's home. Our house was relatively small and there was no room for two active boys, so we were required to stay in our room. There was no radio, TV, video games or computer. The only TV in the house was located in the living room where one of the three pinochle tables for the card party sat. At the time us boys felt the loss of the TV but with only 4 channels we weren't really missing out on much. Most of the homes in our neighborhood still had black and white televisions but since my parents both worked we were lucky enough to have a RCA Color TV.

The seen was now set for the carnige that would occur in our 10 by 10 foot bedroom. Tonight we would have our grandest battle, lots of fun and extreme pain.

After a quick dinner we were escorted to our bedroom and told the only reason we could leave was to the use the bathroom across the hall. By this time Mom and Dad's guests had started to arrive.

Soon the nights events kicked off with a cardboard box. With a large cardboard box who needs TV. We played at being race drivers and airplane pilots while sitting in the box. But this was just the warm up to the grandest adventure of all. We eventually took turns sitting in the box while the other pushed it around and around on the hardwood floor.

Soon we became bored in searched for a game with more adventure, this led us to turning our box into a crash test vehicle. We hoisted the box onto the top bed bunk, then my brother sat in the box feet forward and I gave the box a push. Bam! With a thud my brother struck the floor and rolled out of the box laughing. Seeing what fun it was I then tried the ride.

Not to be out done I tucked three of the flaps down so that just my head stuck out the top. With a harsh laugh my brother gave a vigorous push using all his strength. The box hit the floor with a bam. My ride from the top bunk was faster than his and I landed farther out into the room with a thud. It was a fast and exciting ride.

We each continued to take turns shooting off the bed in the box secure in the knowledge that Dad would be happy we were not fighting. What we did not know was that the sound of the box striking the hardwood floor reverberated through-out the house. Bam! Bam! Bam! Mom and Dad's party guests were becoming concerned. Soon Dad realized he could no longer ignore there comments.

Just as my brother complete his turn and as he rolled free of the box the door banged open, and Dad with a subdued voice so as to not alarm the guests asked "what the hell are you doing!" This time he was taken by surprise as we were playing and not fighting. He stood staring first at one of us then the other, then seeming to make up his mind he said "there will be no more pushing each other off the top bunk, box or no box." With that he exited shutting the door firmly behind him.

After Dad left we got out a board game and tried to play but quickly grew bored. Without the box everything seemed inadequate. My brother sat in the box and looked up to the top bunk. My eyes followed suite. Soon my brother looked down to the bottom bunk and said "Dad didn't saying anything about the bottom bunk". The thought flashed quickly through my mind realizing he was right, it would be alright to use the box from the bottom bunk. Well that suited me just fine as it was my turn and the next ride would be for evens.

We slid the box onto the bottom bunk then I crawled into the box and sat down. Then I had a great idea, why not curl up in the box with my head forward and the top flaps closed. The closed flaps would keep me from falling out of the box, therefore offering protection from the fall. My brother closed the lid of the box then braced his feet against the wall, then with a mighty heave launched me into space.

Everything was dark and there was pain everywhere. I carefully opened one eye to the fierce image of my father standing over me. Everything was blurry but I remember Dad lifting me up to my bunk as I stifled a scream before I lapsed into unconsciousness and sleep.

The next day was Sunday and there were no doctor offices open and it was unheard of to use the hospital. Immediate care facilities were a thing of the future. My shoulder hurt terrible and I had to make do with a temporary sling for my arm until Monday. I didn't sleep well that night and didn't go to school Monday morning.

Dad took me to see our old doctor, Dr. Nautical. When we first moved to Oregon he had still made house calls and I remembered him coming out to examine us in our living room. It was the end of an era.

The previous summer Mom took us in to the doctor's office for an exam and shots. She failed to warn us of the shots. While my brother sat alone in the examination room while Mom was in the waiting room. The nurse returned smiled and left a stray draped with a white towel. We tip toed to the tray and lifted a corner to see a lineup of hypodermic needles. We quickly took it upon ourselves to prevent this tragedy in the making. First we pushed the examination table against the wall. In those days they were open underneath. We then used every movable object in the room to barricade ourselves under the table. When Dr. Nautical entered he glanced under the table and stated in a calm voice that we would have to reschedule for another day. Yes, we won the battle but as we soon learned not the war.

To examine my arm the doctor wanted me down to my skivvies. I tried to undress but had to wait until the nurse came back to help. She was a big nonsense type with a gruff voice that could lead a squad of elite marines, but she proved to be gentle and caused me very little additional pain.

After the exam and x-rays the verdict came back, "broken collar bone". They strapped me into a harness much like a bra without the cups then sent me on my way. In school for the next few weeks I wasn't allowed to play at recess and every time I had to take off or put on my coat the teacher had to help.

The incident with the box led to the first change in living arrangements. My top bunk was lifted off and crowded into the sewing room while my toys and clothes remained in the bedroom I had shared with my brother. I was sleeping better and feeling more rested within a week of moving to the new room until a special on television was aired.

That evening we watched a special on Bigfoot, also known as Sasquatch. Being from the Pacific Northwest where we have had many reports we were all extremely interested to learn more. I did well watching the shows until they started showing reenactments of big foot meeting humans. One in particular lingered, a man in his cabin was in the bathroom sitting on the throne. Bigfoot reaches through the open window and attempts to drag the fellow outside.

This was the beginning of nightmares so severe that Mom and Dad started to notice how exhausted I was. I told them I just couldn't get to sleep and was sure that Bigfoot would reach in through my window to get me. In my mind this was real possibility, even though we lived in a residential neighborhood. I was sure that my first floor window would provide him with the opportunity that he sought.

We moved my bed opposite wall away from the window. This helped but I still could not get to sleep at night. Dad brought in his old radio, 18 inches wide and 12 inches high in a wood case, the inside lined with radio vacuum tubes. When I turned it on the radio would gently hum as the tubes warmed up. Once running I kept the volume almost too low to hear. The old radio was my baby sitter for years humming me to sleep each night.

The old radio is still around and works just as it did then. After I left home Dad kept it in the garage and upon his passing is now in the possession of my brother. Looking at it today is like visiting an old friend that sat with you through a terrible sickness.

With the passing of winter my shoulder had healed and the rains had become less frequent. In early spring Dad had us on top of the garage removing shingles and then removing the sheeting underneath. We would work on it after work/school under a couple of work lights. The lights gave the impression that the roof edge dropped into endless darkness while in reality it was just 10 feet into side yard.

One night it was extra dark and started to drizzle. I kept slipping on the roof and was sure that I would be precipitated into the bottomless darkness below. Starting from this point forward I would slowly become more fearful of falling from a height.

We worked down until we were removing the roof trusses piece by piece. These are similar to trusses used today but each piece was hand cut at the building site to meet the pitch of the roof. At this point we were stepping from the top edge of one board to the next feeling like tight rope walkers. On this day I arrived home from school and had other things I wanted to do that night so I decided to get a head start before Dad got home. You had to step carefully board to board to avoid stepping on the sheet rock witch would give way and precipitate a 12 foot drop to the garage floor.

As I was carefully moving board to board my feet slipped and a dropped astraddle a narrow beam. Both feet had gone through the interior sheet rock and left me riding that narrow beam. I took short fast breaths and tried to concentrate on relieving the pain caused the by the solid blow to my groin. I attempted to push myself up but with my feet through the garage ceiling I could get no leverage. I thought to fall sideways to the next beam but was fearful of causing more damage to the sheet rock. I strained and struggled but to no avail. I shouted for my brother who was watching The Flintstones but he was unable to hear me. I did my best to relieve the pain and waited for rescue.

Soon I hear Dad's truck pull up and saw him get out still in his work uniform. He glanced at the roof but didn't seem to see me. I shrunk waiting for the verbal blast but truly in such terrible pain that I was ready to face anything. I heard Dad open the garage door and new he couldn't fail to notice the addition of a pair of converse sneakers.

True to form I soon heard him swearing and shouting as he made his way to the ladder at the side of the house. I could tell he was angry beyond belief and braced for my corporal punishment though getting off my tenders would be a relief. Dad was behind me when he reached the top of the ladder and I couldn't see him. But what I heard was nearly as bad, silence. Then I hear a low chuckle that became a laugh. He was quite upset and while I didn't receive any corporal punishment in the years to come he would tell the story to friends and relatives with gusto and great laughs.

The frame and trusses went up quickly as they were preordered and lifted into place by the crane on the delivery truck. 24 feet from the front of the house witch was actually the front of the garage and 16 feet wide. The adult neighbor was enlisted to help with the siding on the second floor . My brother and I setup saw horses to rest each piece of siding upon then would race to see who could paint the most on the sheet. Before reaching the last sheet we were each covered in olive green paint.

Two windows were installed, one in back (my bedroom) and the other in front. I was anxious to try out the new bedroom even though there was no electricity, insulation or sheet rock. I setup an army cot in the center of the room and blissful drifted off to sleep. It was summer so the unfinished room was more comfortable at night but blistering hot during the day.

Eventually nearly everything was completed. There was one large room each with its own closet and shelves. My brother slept near the front and myself at the back. This arrangement worked for a while and provided a large space in the middle where we could spend time playing games with friends and wrestling.

Mom purchased stick on carpet squares, bright electric blue and red. They made an exotic checkerboard pattern on the floor that fit with the theme of the 1970s but could also cause dizziness on occasion.

Eventually a point was reached where we each wanted our own separate rooms. The fighting had reached a point again where we need a wall between us. Dad placed a wall between us and a short hallway; each room had its own door. He was clever about the construction and blended in as if it had been the original plan.

I was very happy in my room. We were a long way from my parents' bedroom and isolated where we could make noise and banging without disturbing the card parties. Best of all, the second floor was well beyond the reach of Big Foot.

CHAPTER 12

Camping on the Salmonberry River

We had a wonderful and very private camp site we used with permission from the owner. The turn off was West of Elsie Oregon on Highway 26. We always remembered it as there was a tall statue of Paul Bunyan and Babe the blue ox at the store. Today there is a sign with Paul Bunyan painted on it.

We followed the Nehalem River and passed through Henry Rierson Spruce Run Campground. Then continue for a few more miles to the Salmonberry River where we would turn off onto a small narrow unpaved road with a gate. Often this road was blocked or covered by debris so we would clear its 2 mile length with shovels and saws as part of our contribution to using the campground. Today the road is heavily overgrown and washed out in place.

At the end of the road is a grassy area that slopes gently down to the Salmonberry River. The river at this point is 30 feet across and up to 8 feet deep in places. The water runs clear and pristine between stone covered banks. Across the river were seldom used railroad tracks. There were three camping sites, we would usually have the campground to ourselves, but other people that visited were always quiet and polite.

After setting up the old canvas tent and sleeping bags we would go down to the river take a dip in the cold water. Later we would get out our inner tubes and spend the day walking up the creek and then floating down the river. There are Newts or as some people call them salamanders in shallow pools along the shore. The newts have dark brown backs and an orange stomach that is specific to this Northwest species (Genus Taricha). We would spend hours capturing the newts and placing them in walled off enclosures made with stones.

When a train did come by it was fascinating to first hear its rumble, then it would come into view as if popping out from between the trees. We would raise our hands and give the universal sign to blow the horn. Engineers always waved and would toot their horns much to our delight.

Several years later Dad decided there must be great hunting along the tracks so he built a railway cart. This was a reinforced board with four wheels. One wheel was connected to a lawnmower engine and supplied power to spin the wheel.

One Fall weekend my brother and Father took the cart deer hunting. They had great fun until they heard a train, this was when they found out the platform was too heavy to move quickly. The story had a happy ending and after the train passed they continued hunting.

After the using the tent a few time my father decided to build a camper. First thing I knew of it was a wooden frame in the garage that someone had built using 2x2 lumber. Dad covered it in aluminum sealing the seams with rubber gaskets. Inside he built a small kitchen and cupboard while against the front was a table and bench seats to sit four people. The portion over the truck cab was used by my brother and I while the table was converted into a bed for Mom and Dad. It was all very cozy and comfortable and most importantly light enough that a couple of people could slide it into the bed of our old Chevrolet truck.

We kept it in our back yard up on a couple of stands that made it easy to load onto the truck. My brother and I anxious to try it out decided to sleep over one night in the back yard. We both climbed into the cabover section and nestled into our sleeping bags and fell fast asleep. In the middle of the night I awoke to a light in my face with my father looking down on me through the door. My bewildered mind finally grasp the fact that I was on the floor of the camper. My father then asked me what I was doing on the floor. He had heard a tremendous crash and ran out to make sure we were ok. I was indeed on the floor having rolled off the overhead, struck the table then rolled off onto the floor. I never awoke during the fall and was unharmed.

The next year we headed up to the Salmonberry river campground with our camper and the four of us crowded into the front seat of the old truck. We noted that someone had been in ahead of us with equipment and cleared the road and filled in the pot holes. It was a nice road now quite improved and better yet for the first time we didn't have to clear the road ourselves. When we arrived at the campground there were two groups of campers there ahead of us witch left the one less desirable spot. Dad decided that instead of using this spot he would back the truck down onto the rocky beach of smooth rounded boulders. He backed in carefully until we were in partial shade and 15 feet from the edge of the river. This was great spot and we enjoyed the next couple of days participating in our normal activities. On the third day the owner of the property came out to speak with my father. It was not good news. He was the new owner and wanted out today as he was having a large family reunion on the spot. Dad argued extensively with him but in the end we had to leave.

Mom climbed into the truck cab and Dad behind the wheel. Still in our swimming suits, my brother and I climbed into the camper and closed the door. We sat at the dinette as Dad through the old truck into first gear. Dad must have still been angry because he put his foot down quickly shifting from first to second gear and we lurched up and over the boulders the truck swinging precariously first on one side and then the other. We hung on for dear life bouncing up and down on the seats. As he made the last turn and pulled onto the road the pantry cabinet burst open and three new glass bottles of ketchup escaped and smashed on the floor spraying a sticky red mess across the camper and onto us boys.

We pounded on the wall to get Dad's attention, after a moment he came to a stop. We could hear his cursing as it burned the air around him. Mom was first to the camper door and opened it to what looked like a bloody mess. Mom turned white as a sheet and a gasp escaped her lips. My brother and I still bare foot in our swim trunks splattered with the red ketchup. Mom to choked up to speak did not say a word but I could now clearly hear Dad's voice running at high volume expressing his displeasure at having to stop.

Dad stood at the camper door, from where I sat it seemed like his eyes pop from his head, then his mouth drop opened. It was fear I'm sure, this from a man who had never shown fear to us boys. Alarm that his boys had been severely injured. He recovered after a moment but now much calmer and made sure we were not hurt. But true to his nature the next question was why didn't we stop the bottles, what could I say. Dad you were driving like a crazy man, I left my thoughts unspoken and just shook my head. After cleaning up the mess we complete our departure from the Salmon Berry river camp site for the last time.

We ended back on Highway 26 where we thought our vacation was over and we would be headed for home. Dad had other ideas, he turned left and we were on our way to the Oregon coast. We found an open campground and remained there for the rest of the week. We had fun at the beach collecting shells and camping in the state campground. Dad even made an exception and took the truck onto the beach where we drove down the beach and stopped for the day to play in the sand and surf. We rode on the sand buggies across the Oregon dunes in a large open topped bus where the driver took us straight down a near vertical slope as a finally. All the time Dad was unexpectedly kind and saw to it that us boys were having fun. It was a great vacation despite the unexpected mishaps.

CHAPTER 13

The Christmas with Roger and Jennifer

Mom and Dad helped out there friends over the years. The 70's were an era of you scratch my back I'll scratch yours. Today this seems to have mostly passed as observed by the number of times I have helped people out but when comes to me needing help any excuse with do.

Mom and Dad had friends living in Hillsboro from England that returned to the mother country to frequently spend time with their friends and relatives. Mom had met Mrs. Wilson in the legal secretary organization one hot summer during one of their sessions in Bend Oregon. At this session they were seated on the bleachers in the gymnasium when the event that drew them together occurred.

All of the doors of the gymnasium were opened when in jogged a young man wearing nothing but a pair of cowboy boots, cowboy hat and a big smile. As the group of woman stared he tipped his hat and exited out the other side of the gym.

During the time Mr. and Mrs. Wilson returned to England they would leave there children Roger and Jennifer with my parents. Roger was the older brother and Jennifer his sister two years younger. My brother and I were several years older and that past summer and had earned a modest income babysitting the two of them during the summer vacation.

Originally Roger and Jennifer lived in Hillsboro Oregon within bicycling distance. But at some point the family moved to Barrow Alaska where there father became the school principle and mother the school secretary. Those that live in Barrow and have means leave during the summer for warmer weather in the lower 48. Barrow is north of the Arctic Circle located on a peninsula that juts out into the Arctic ocean. This makes it the northernmost city in the USA. The town has a population of slightly over 4000. The climate is categorized as Polar, with 160 days below zero Fahrenheit.

This particular Christmas break while Mr. and Mrs. Wilson traveled to England for the holidays, Roger and Jennifer came to stay with us and join in our Christmas holiday. I often felt this was extremely unfortunate as Jennifer's birthday falls two days after Christmas.

This Christmas in 1972 Roger and Jennifer arrived to spend Christmas with our family. That year like many in Oregon was wet with no snow. We setup down stairs family room for Roger to sleep in and the guest bedroom for Jennifer.

After they settled in we drove out to a Christmas tree farm nearby. We came home muddy from traipsing across the fields and cutting down our own tree. While tieing the tree to the top of the old chevy it started to rain. I grumbled as I crossed to the other side of the car with the rope where my grumbles disappeared. In the Eastern sky was the most beautiful rainbow I had ever seen against a background of black clouds. Each color was bright and vibrant, not the washed out color normally seen. As I watched a second rainbow formed below the first equally vibrant. To this day the only rainbow I have seen to compete was a fire rainbow in Idaho and the that one was not as brightly colored.

That night we decorated the Christmas tree with lights, ornaments and strings of tinsel. Mom brought out the Christmas stockings and placed them on the fireplace hearth. Our two Siamese cats as usual chased each other through the boxes. My mother who always seemed prepared for anything, had stockings she hung for Jennifer and Roger. On Christmas morning they would find them stuffed with small treats and small toys.

That evening we sat down to dinner as a family and after prayers dug in. It was at this point that we hear a loud alarm going off. It grew from low to loud and repeated itself. The hairs on the back of my neck rose as I saw my mother bolt from the table. Abruptly the sound halted and we each stared back and forth waiting for what! We could not be sure. Momentarily Mom came back into dinning room from the laundry room. I immediately thought it must have been the washer or dryer making that awful noise. But all other thought were forgotten as I realized that Mom had my cat Missy in her arms.

Right before we had sat down for dinner Mom had pulled some cloths from the dryer and tossed in another load. She said it only took a moment. In the poor lighting of the laundry room Missy had hopped into the nice warm dryer to inevitably taken a terrifying dryer ride. Missy while shook up, appeared uninjured. That night she rested in my lap during TV time and by morning was back to her old antics.

Christmas was still a few days away and we filled the days decorating the house and cleaning the house for Christmas dinner with my relatives. Two members of my father's family Hugh and Don were also living in Oregon and with the families together it was always a three turkey dinner.

On Christmas morning I was abruptly awaken by the sound of a blow horn. I could clearly hear the person manning the horn who was shouting out "Roger, come out before anyone gets harmed". Roger I thought, He should be down stairs asleep. Since I couldn't see who was doing the shouting from my back yard window I rushed to the front window in my brothers room. There I found my brother staring out the window and pointing into the street.

Below on the street were several police cars and a large black panel van with the letters SWAT on the side. As we watched the door opened and out poured men dressed in black wearing bullet proof vests, helmets and automatic weapons. They charged down the side yard on either side of the house. Oh man Roger you have really done it now.

We ran back to my bedroom to watch the SWAT team line up along the back fence facing toward the neighbor's house. I remember thinking, Roger you have really blown Christmas now, only coal in your stocking. As I watched I realized it must be something else going on. A different Roger would be fine be me.

I ran down the stairs and into the family room. Roger was sound asleep. Dad appeared in the dining room with his bath robe draped over his shoulders but hanging open. With typical Dad response in a very loud whisper he asked "what the blazes are you doing." I told him about the swat team and police while we walked through the family room to the back sliding doors. He saw the SWAT members and nodded his head sagely while our Roger continued to sleep in the bed next to us.

All of this went on for quite some time with the man yelling through the blow horn and the SWAT team in our back yard. Finally from the house behind we saw a man walk towards the street with his arms in the air. A police officer ran forward and locked his hands behind his back. It was over. Roger and Jennifer didn't wake up for another half hour and didn't believe us when we told the story.

Later I learned that the man had barricaded himself in the house and fired a shotgun. He was threatening to shoot himself when the negotiator arrived to talk him out of the house. All of it is really quit sad to think that someone would be so lonely on Christmas day when so many are ready to welcome them into their homes on Christmas.

CHAPTER 14

First trip to Vermont

D o you remember you first grade teacher? Mine was Mrs. Peach and she was no peach. She was very strict but as far as I remember got the job done. One of her favorite tricks was to drop a pin, it we didn't hear it hit the floor she lectured us on being quiet then cancelled recess to make her point.

Mrs. Shoe was my second grade teacher and not a very nice, what she did have was a violent temper. She had a bucket next to her desk full of yard sticks. She needed a lot of them because she busted a lot of them on the back sides of her students. During one incident she broke three sticks chasing a girl around the class room as the girl screamed and cried. The little yard sticks meant nothing to me, my father used a rubber hose. Overall second grade was unpleasant but things were about to get better.

Dad took me to the optometrist Dr. Furie that year. Dr. Furie confirmed that I was near sighted, he also explained why I couldn't see the black board. Dr. Furie was an integral part of my life and was the person that convinced me that I should go back to college after dropping out for two years. Dr. Furie was a wonderful man that had a positive influence on my life.

When I returned to class the kids started to pick on me about my glasses but fortunately Dr. Furie had prepared me. When they called me four eyes I would look at them making eye contact, pull off my glasses and stare at them before I started counting. Two lens in my glasses and two eyeballs for a grand total of four. I would then look them straight in the eyes again and say "Hey you're right; I do have four eyes, cool"! This always seemed to surprise the name callers and took the starch out of any leverage they thought they would gain through bulling

The summer after second grade I attended summer school where I was able to catch-up quickly on the learning I missed why viewing the world through a blur. The Third grade went much better and each year after.

During third grade I started to play marbles, they were making a huge resurgence at the time. Kids carried there marbles in sacks and gathered on the playground at lunch to compete. Steelies became a coveted item, better known as ball barring's. We mentioned this to Dad and he was supplied us with an endless supply from his work. The ball bearings were seconds that they would otherwise recycle. We eventually flooded the market and smashed untold glass marbles.

The summer after third grade was when we made our first trip to Vermont as a family. My first trip just Mom and I went. I was 3 months old and we made the trip with the to visit her parents. I was shown off as there first grandchild. Obviously I don't remember the trip, only a couple photos of Mom and I climbing the steps to board the airplane.

Our first family trip occurred when I was 8 years old and my brother 7. Flying on Delta airlines jet we had a blast, first stop Chicago then onto

Burlington Vermont. The flight attendants were really nice and we were served a lunch during the flight. The pilots let us boys stand at the open cockpit door and watch them fly the plane after which they awarded us with our wings. But the most fascinating thing was found by my brother at the back of the plane. We both crowded into the restroom where he showed me jet engine type flush of the toilet.

I wasn't entirely sure what this trip was about, well vacation but not like anything we had done before. We were not aware that we had a whole bunch of relatives living in Vermont. Mom and Dad had left Vermont in 1957 for a job in California.

Turned out the trip was to visit relatives. My father had 7 brothers and sisters and my mother has 7 brothers and sisters. All told it ended up being 27 Aunts and uncles as one of my uncles had not yet married. Not to mention the masses of cousins and great uncles and aunts.

At Chicago O'Hare there was an extended wait. The airport screening procedure was much simpler than todays and the screeners let my brother and I stand in the booth with the operator watching the x-ray screen. The operator pointed to one bag and we could see it was completely crammed with bottles. He told us lots of people fill up on liquor for their return trip home. We used the airport as our personal playground dashing back and forth as we visited every store in the terminal.

The finally leg of the journey brought us into Burlington Vermont. This is a relatively small airport and much quieter then Chicago. Waiting for us were an older man and woman I recognized as my mother's parents. They had visited the previous year at our home in Hillsboro. My mother hugged and kissed them both. This was my Grandfather and Grandmother, my mother's parents (Cornelius and Evelyn).

Grandpa Cornelius drove us east to their small farm house in Wolcott, the highway on our route cut through large rock ridges of granite and rolling pastures and farms. The majority of the trip was on the freeway but we turned off onto a two lane highway for the last hour. Along this highway is Ben and Jerry's ice cream factory. They started business in 1978 which was still 12 years away.

The red farm hose sits on a rubble stone foundation and has been added onto several times over the years. There were only three bedrooms, the two smallest were used by my uncles and aunts but were now left vacant. Five boys had lived in one bedroom and three girls the other. My brother and I shared one of these small bedrooms during our visit. The property had been a farm for several generations. My grandfather converted it to a gravel quarry and very little of the 75 acres still exists. The Barn was still full of farming implements but no longer used.

That first night we forced ourselves to stay up so that we could listen to the adults talk in the living room. But before long we were sleeping sitting up. We were sent to our bedroom up stairs where we both fell into bed sleeping fully clothed through the night.

Grandpa Cornelius warned us not to play in the old barn as it was dangerous. This became distressingly clear several years later. Two of my adult uncles at the request of Grandpa were sent out to take down the barn, a daunting task. Looking for the quickest way to complete the job, they hooked a chain to the tractor with the other end hooked to a large beam. They made sure all of the connections were tight and started to pull with the tractor, the old barn shuttered from top to bottom as they gave the chain a tug with the tractor. Then in slow motion the side wall started to topple towards them. My Uncles were on the jump and ran away from the barn leaving the tractor to its fate. The barn continued to shutter, then groaned as each wall in turn dropped to the ground. When the dust settled, they looked back to see not a single wall, beam or rafter standing. It was a narrow escape.

Water for the house came from a spring three quarters of a mile away. When Grandpa said he was going to check on the spring we were ready. The pipe to the spring went under the busy road in front of their house across a huge pasture, along the bottom of a river 40 feet across then up the hillside. When we got there he lifted the cover and we were looking into a rock lined hole with clear water gentle bubbling into the pool. The feed from the spring had originally used wooden pipes but Grandpa with some of his sons had replaced it with metal pipes several years previously.

A few years later they had a hard winter and when the thaw started there were problems with flooding and ice buildup on bridge pylons. The standard procedure was for the county to drill a hole in the ice and drop in packets of dynamite set with timers. The explosive load would float under the ice and explode breaking the ice and creating a channel for the water to flow through. The pipe to the spring was doomed as a packet of dynamite blew next to the pipe.

Grandpa had a well company come out and drill in the backyard; they hit granite at 30 feet, broke through the shelf and hit water immediately afterward. Where we live in Oregon this is almost unheard, Wells are typically deeper than 150 feet.

The day of the family reunion arrived for my mother's side of the family. We had met a handful of aunts, uncles and cousins but eventually they arrived in droves and stayed for the day. We were feeling board until my Uncle David showed up. He was the last remaining bachelor of the family, soon we were rough housing in the house and Grandma sent us all out side where we wrestled and chased my uncle for the next hour. Later there was food and drinks, no alcohol or beer, Grandma wouldn't have it. The rest of the afternoon was spent hanging out with the cousins, all younger then I being the first born grandchild. Some of the adults gathered around Grandpa's horse shoe pits and played until the light failed.

The next day Dad and us boys drove over to Lake Elmore and then down to the farm that my father had grown up on. Unlike Mothers folks this farm was still active raising dairy cattle. We met my father's mother, Grandma Lena and my aunt and uncle (Barb and Harold). Barb was one of Dad's older sisters who lived on the farm and operated the dairy along with their son Bud. Bud was much older then I and strong from working the farm. At this writing sadly the farm is no longer farming but is still managed by Bud as Crossview Gardens. Crossview has a huge flower garden with day lilies and hostas as the core flowers. They have done a wonderful job with the farm, a search of the web tells you that they are open in July and August for viewing by the public.

The old farm house on the site is where my Grandpa Jesse and Grandma Lena raised 8 children, two girls and 6 boys. Next to the farm house was a small home where my grandmother Lena lived.

Dad took us into meet our Grandma Lena for the first time, his father Jesse had passed away near the time of my birth. She was a sweet woman that gave us leave to run and play around the property why she and Dad talked. Her health was not good but then she was quite a bit older then my mother's parents having been born 20 years before my Grandpa Cornelius.

We walked around the farm house and looked out at the Holstein cows in the pasture then across the gravel road to the dairy barn. We peaked into the milking parlor where there was a large stainless steel container, then we walked the length of the barn looking at the head stalls and gear used for milking the cows. The barn had the aroma of fresh cow manure overlaid by the smell of hay. We found the ladder to the hay loft and there we played with the kittens living there.

While exploring the hay bales and admiring the smooth worn floor created by decades of hay bales we heard the cows coming into be milked. We peaked down from the loft as the huge animals came in and each found there spot. Each time all 50 cows would make their way to the same spots where they received custom blends of grains and could slurp water out of metal bows permanently affixed to the barn. The water bowls were fascinating in that no matter how much a cow drank there would always seem to be more water. I peaked in a bowl and saw a paddle in the bottom, when I pressed upon it more water flowed into the bowl.

We watched as Uncle Harold and Cousin Bud milked the cows. They were using a automatic milker, they would first sanitize the cows utters then plug the milking bucket in to the vacuum line overhead. There were long rubber cups attached that were attached to each of the teats on the cow. The rubber cups anxiously sucked up tightly and began gently to remove the milk from the cow. When done they would disconnect the machine and moved to the next cow. When the milker was full Bud hauled it into the milking parlor where the larger stainless steel container sat. He poured the milk into the container called a pasteurizer then went back to milk more cows.

The afternoon was getting late and evening was coming on as the cows were released. Each in turn walked out the back door. They would be back and read at 4 AM the next morning.

We walked over the Grandma Lena's house where Dad and her were still firmly engrossed in conversation. Back in her front yard we found an old bathtub sunk into the earth with gold fish swimming about. It was about then I bug flew up on to my brothers arm with his back side glowing; this was a first for us as fireflies are uncommon where we live. We ran to the door and Grandma admired our bug, she called it a lightening bug. Grandma stepped away and came back with a jar. The yard was lighting up with the fireflies and we gathered as many as we could into the old mason jar.

All too soon Dad came out to let us know we needed to return to Grandma Evelyn's. We released the fireflies and all to soon found ourselves on our way. We had missed dinner at Grandma Evelyn's house so Dad stopped at the burger stand in Morrisville. He ordered us Cokes, fries and hamburgers with everything. We had quite and eye opener that day. In Oregon when you order everything on a burger you get ketchup, mustard, lettuce, onions and tomato. In Morrisville everything means bun, patty and ketchup, the regular burger has no ketchup. But on the other had a large Coke wasn't 16 ounces but 32 ounces.

On the day of my mother's family reunion at Grandma Evelyn's house, all of my uncles, aunts and cousins came as well as some great uncles and aunts. There were more than 30 people attending and we had great fun meeting all of our cousins for the first time. In the afternoon several adults migrated to Grandpa's horse shoe pits where they played until it started to become dark. That night I sat on the front porch with my Grandpa, a rare moment, as he always seemed to resent my presence. My Grandma always appeared to enjoy my company so spent quite a bit of time together.

Several years later I visited Vermont with my new wife and our baby boy. Again we stayed with Grandma Evelyn as she wouldn't have it any other way. The next morning after we arrived I was up early and Grandma asked if I wanted to go along with Grandpa to check on the cemetery maintenance. I was out the door to Grandpa's small pickup truck. I asked him if I could go along, "sure he replied, going to make the rounds". I opened the passenger door where his dog Rufus was sitting, slid partway in the picked up Rufus to hold him on my lap. That's as far as I got, with an angry snarl Grandpa said "that's where Rufus sits, you will have to sit on the floor"! I looked at the small floor of the mini pickup, gave it a brief thought then dismissed the idea. I looked up at my Grandpa where I was meant by an angry snarl from his bright red face. What could I say?

I shut the door and walked back to the house understanding for the first time my role in Grandfathers life. There is no time in my life for people with distorted values.

The next day Dad drove is back to the dairy farm and Grandma Lena. Along the way we saw a large round barn. It was a beautiful yellow with white trim sitting in the middle of a luscious green pasture. Three years later the barn burned to the ground. The fire caused by green hay bales (green hay with its high moisture content can spontaneously combust into an extremely hot fire.) The high moisture content builds heat and causes a chemical reaction that starts the fire. The bales of hay stacked closely together insulates the inner bales, so the larger the number of bales the more likely they will combust.

On the shores of Lake Elmore is where my Grandma Lena and Grandpa Jesse grew up. Grandpa Jesse spent parts of his winters cutting, extracting and stacking blocks of ice. This ice in turn was used for kitchen ice boxes and any place where cooling during the warmer summer months was needed.

Vermont is a green state with rolling hills, small mountains with pastures and fields bordered by stone fences. If you find yourself visiting the green hills of Vermont be prepared to find your own path. A typical response to a request for directions, "Yah can't get there from here". If you're from the west where we travel great distances be prepared for a new concept of distance. Once on a drive with my wife we asked if it was far to Montpelier, the capitol of Vermont. The response was it's a very long drive; you won't want to go that far for a drive. I drive further to do our grocery shopping, it took us less than an hour and only that long because we made so many stops to view sites.

We stopped at my Uncle Almeran's house to pick up a fishing pole. He lives a short way down the road from Grandma Lena. He made his living as a mobile mechanic fixing equipment in barns and fields. He was also talented at building ponds, evidence of his work can still be found in the area.

We headed down across the lower pasture to a very tiny brook or in western vernacular creek. It was so small I could easily hop across it then back with both feet together. Spread out along the creek were small pools where Dad hoped to catch a fish. As we approached the creek Dad had us get down on hands and knees and carefully creep up to the bank. He then used his pole to dangle the line over a small pool hardly two feet across. It took no time at all and a beautiful trout snapped up the bait, he was all of 14 inches and you could have knocked me over with a feather. To this day my brother and I can still hardly believe that such a large fish lived in such as small creek.

After fishing we wandered to the bottom of the pasture where dad showed us a tree that had a wad of rocks and nails imbedded in the bark. This was the remains of mischief that my father and his brother had created. Next we walked through a grove of sugar maple trees. Deep in the trees was the sugar shack where they collected and boiled maple syrup. Peeping in the door we could see a large 8 foot long, 4 foot wide pan where the sap was boiled. Nothing was being boiled until the spring when the sap would flow.

That night instead of returning to my other Grandma Evelyn's house, my brother and I stayed at Grandma Lena's farm. Aunt Barb put us up in a comfortable small bedroom upstairs above the kitchen, the same room my father had shared with Uncle Don growing up. The next morning my aunt awoke us at 4 AM to help get the cows in for milking. We brought the cows down from the upper pasture stumbling along half awake. After milking we were back to the house for breakfast.

After breakfast my aunt Jessica showed up on the door step. This was the first time I remember meeting her, one of her daughters would move to Seattle with her husband a few years later making it convenient for us to visit back and forth. The two aunts saddle the horses and a pony to ride. After directions on how to ride we headed up the road for a cool morning ride through the country side. I felt just like a cowboy and to think I had to come from cowboy country to Vermont for this experience. We met with a local farmer and helped herding his cows down the road and to a new pasture. My Aunts and I had a pleasant morning. That day each of them captured a part of my heart.

After the horseback ride there was a big family reunion with my father's side of the family. Aunt Barb served maple syrup on snow even though it was summer time. She boiled the maple syrup until it started to thicken then poured amber streams of it over the snow.

The next morning at Grandma Evelyn's house she taught us how to crochet and in between she showed us how to play the piano. Grandma's freezer was kept in the garage filled with popsicles, ice cream sandwiches and frozen candy bars. Grandma Evelyn treated it like an open bar and it was thoroughly enjoyed by the grandchildren.

Dad took us to the cemetery in Morrisville Vermont to visit our Grandpa Jesse's grave site. We found the stone and while the others wondered around looking for family members I sat by my Grandfathers grave and felt grief at his passing. I had never met him as he died two months before my birth. Even to this day the memory of his death causes me great sadness. I don't know why, only that I feel something of great importance should have occurred but never did.

A few years later we visited Vermont again. On the evening of July 20th 1969 I was sitting next to my grandmother Evelyn watching Neil Armstrong walk on the moon. Several years after this I met my bride to be at Oregon State University and that date become more significant as July 20th is my wife's birthday.

My brother and I were saddened to leave Vermont. We could feel farming in our blood and Vermont was where we would plan to farm. Through missed chances and the vagrancies of life we never owned a farm but I always remember pouring over a farm catalog head to head with my brother as we planned each detail of our farm.

CHAPTER 15

Learning to cook

My brother and I learned to cook by television we joined many others to watch Graham Kerr dash about his kitchen to prepare gourmet dishes. The dash leads one to understand the name of his show, The Galloping Gourmet. The cooking shows of the 1960's had a significant impact on our approaches to cooking, others that impacted our methods were greats such as Jacque Pepin and Julia Childs.

Home alone on school vacations provided the perfect venue for us to experiment with cooking. With limited supervision we took to the kitchen that leads to our misadventures.

One June morning at the start of summer vacation I awoke to a delightful smell. This was not usual as during the summers my brother and I relied on cold cereal for our breakfast. Dressing quickly and taking the steps two at a time I jumped and grabbed the chin up bar my father had installed. A couple of years earlier I had not been able to perform more than a couple pull-ups for my physical fitness test. After months of working out I could do over 50 pull ups and then 5 of what Dad called skinning the cat. What you ask is this: hang from the bar and bring your feet up over your head, then between your arms. Keep going until your feet are again pointed at the floor. Then reverse the process while never letting go of the bar.

I dropped to the floor and continued through the laundry room to arrive in the kitchen where my younger brother was cooking. He had a stack of crepes 6 inches tall, this was a lot of crepes. He would pour a bit of batter in the pan and swish it around, as it bubbled he quickly flipped it to finish the other side. I begged for a taste and he allowed as I could have one, wow how delicious. I reached for another but was cut off and informed I would need to make my own. The previous day we had watched Graham Kerr on the Galloping Gourmet make crepes so I knew the technique but needed the recipe. My brother showed me the recipe in the cookbook and I was off, making my own stack of crepes.

After the crepes cook off I decided to try more recipes and since I loved cookies I pulled out Mom's cookie cook book and thumbed through the recipes. While trying to decide I wandered into the family room with the cookie book to watch the Julia Childs cooking show. While I watched my Siamese cat Missy climbed in my lap and made herself comfortable. I set the cookbook aside to give her some attention and to listen to the rumble of her purr. She was a friendly cat and would go to anyone for a pet. I had a special bond with her such that she would abandon any other lap for mine.

For lunch that day I decided to experiment with the Campbell's canned tomato soup. We didn't have much for spices beyond Salt and Pepper so I added some tobasco sauce and mustard. I liked it but wished I had more spices. The next Christmas we remedied this by purchasing Mom the spice rack she wanted. This would be my spice training ground

, I learned to judge the usage of each spice based on the smell, experience and recipes.

Next day started my covert cookie trials began in earnest. My first attempt was sugar cookies, no instructions for me, I just tossed all the ingredient in a bowl and beat the daylights out of it. When it was to dry I added water until it looked like cookie dough. Once baked the sugar cookies were flat and thin like crackers, I judged them to be a failure. The neighbor boys that came by judged them tasty. Afterwards carefully cleaned the kitchen and put everything away so that I wouldn't get in trouble. Little did I know how wrong I would prove to be.

That summer I continued my methods of trial and error to perfect the art of baking cookies when I wasn't otherwise engaged in summer activities such as swimming, bike riding and baseball. The neighborhood had a significant lack of girls but a large population of boys.

One hot summer day us boys hopped on our bikes wearing our swim suits and carrying a towel. We took the 2 mile ride across town to the Hillsboro swimming pool. We arrived at the pool, paid Mrs. Weinger our 25 cents, dropped our towels in the locker room, took a quick shower and were into the pool. The wonderful part of the pool on a hot day was that it was not heated. It was delightfully cool rectangle starting at 3 feet and going to 10 feet at the other end where there was a low and high diving board.

We weren't very skilled divers but made up for it with our enthusiasm and belly flops. The high board was a challenge for several of us. My technique was to walk to the end looking forward but not down then hop off the end. During an earlier attempt I made it up the ladder and became alarmed at the height from the ground. I shivered and tried to back down the ladder but there were already several kids waiting. I walked to the middle and made the unforgivable mistake of looking down. Now I really wanted back down and shouted at the kids on the ladder to reverse direction but to no avail. I finally sucked in a big breath of air and started back to the middle of the board ready to give it my all or nothing. Still holding my breath I decided on a quick approach so I ran down the board but before long slipped on the board bounced on my back side and slid head first toward the water. I'm still holding my breath as I hit the water, my breath shoots out and I take in a big lung full of water as I plunged toward the bottom. I came up feeling more dead, than alive in front of the life guard who made sure I didn't need help. This event kept me off the high board for a while, the vision of the concrete edge of the pool I barely missed providing nightmares for several weeks.

They whistled everyone out of the pool around 6 PM, we walked towards the locker room and saw Dad sitting on a bench in the shade. He told the group of us it was OK to continue swimming. Eventfully the pool lights came on as it started to get dark but still we played on, the pool completely ours at this point. I wouldn't know until later that Dad had come in and rented the pool after talking to Mrs. Weinger who was a mother of three Boy Scouts in our troop.

Afterwards Dad piled us eight boys and our bikes into the back of his pickup and took us to Artic circle where we had burgers, fries and ice cream cones. My father was very popular with the neighborhood boys that night. Over the years Dad would rent the pool several times on hot days.

My first successful attempt at cookies came with a package of Nestle chocolate chips I found in the bottom of the freezer. I finally reasoned that I should read the recipe and follow the directions. The cookies came out great and I shared them with the other neighborhood kids. They were a great success and spurred me on to greater challenges. I still lacked some of the basic skills to make challenging recipes a success. No doubt I was on my way.

That night as we all sat down to dinner my mother asked if us boys knew what was happening to the flour and sugar. She had gone to use it and found the containers nearly empty and thought she had forgotten to purchase more. The next trip to the store she had purchased more and it too had disappeared. She was now concerned so I confessed to baking while she and Dad were away. I had knew this day would come though I had hoped it would not.

Mom's thought our cooking was exciting and encouraged us to do more. Dad's response was disastrous. With a grin on his face he said since we were cooking we could start preparing dinner every night. Dad taught us how to make all of the New England dishes that he knew plus a few more. Salmon wiggle, Shepard's pie, stew, liver and onions, meat loaf and so forth. We ate salmon frequently; all of it caught fishing the waters of the Pacific ocean near our home. For us it was the hamburger of the day, I don't understand people that act like it is a rare treat. Another staple was venison and elk that we hunted and caught ourselves.

Hash was Friday's dinner, we unearthed the hand meat grinder and attached it to the cutting board. Then all the left overs for the week were brought from the refrigerator and ground together, you name it, meatloaf, salmon, liver, baked potatoes, carrots. We would then dump this into a well-oiled skillet, pack in down and wait until the bottom turned brown. All of this drove me to try new recipes to escape our daily fair.

Us boys made dinner frequently though thankfully not every night and then cleaned up afterwards washing the dishes by hand. My brother soon had a severe and painful rash on his hands and arms, the conclusion by the doctor, "he's allergic to the soap". Brother enjoyed no having to do the dishes, occasionally he would help while wearing gloves but it could still be a problem.

I took cooking classes in Junior high school that fall and soon was experimenting on my family with such things as omelets and quiche. But some of my greatest lessons learned were in Boy Scouts cooking over an open fire.

The trick to cooking over a fire is coals. Get a good fire going adding some heavy pieces of wood and let them burn down to coals. Your water will boil faster and you have greater control over your pans temperature. Mr. West our Scout Master also worked us hard policing cooking areas to prevent accidents and he was always there with his trademark phrase "It's burned just the way I like it". This was said with utmost sincerity and varied only in the verb burned.

While on an overnight back pack trip on Eagle Creek trail located in the Columbia Gorge we had an accident that could have been prevented. Mr. West had just scolded us about being careful and if your not cooking to stay out of the way when Robert strolled by the fire. Robert's boots were untied with the tongue hanging open and shoe laces dragging. On his trip by the fire the laces caught the cooking bacon pan with all that wonderful grease. Before our eyes the pan flipped through the air and landed on his boot spilling all that hot grease down the front of his foot. Robert moved as though launched like a rocket, landing in the cold water of Eagle creek. Catastrophe averted and lesson learned.

In all the years of cooking over open fires in pine and fir forests I have never had an problems with fires spreading and we always made sure our fires were out and cool to the touch before leaving. While on a trip with a friend we took a back packers camp stove as open fires were forbidden in the area. The first night we cleared a space for the stove and set it up for cooking. I started the stove while Bob went to get fresh water. With the stove burning I turned to get out my pots and pans then turning to see the undergrowth on fire four feet from the stove. I turned back to my back pack and pulled out my portable shovel and worked to put the fire out. To this day I never trust a camp stove.

Over the years I have cooked on back packing adventures on Mount Rainier, Mount Hood, Mount Jefferson and in many other wilderness areas in the Cascade mountains and my skill with cooking over an open fire has been a skill put to good use. No freeze dried meals or Kraft Macaroni and cheese for me, I put together great tasting meals that enhances the back packing experience.

CHAPTER 16

Linoleum Kittens

When a young boy, my brother Mark and I had two beautiful Siamese kittens. Candy a rich dark seal point and Cocoa a dark blue point. Siamese kittens have beautiful blue eyes and playful personalities. They loved racing through the house, climbing the drapes or chasing everything tantalizing bits of string.

During the kitten stage I helped Dad who was building an family room onto our home. Dad was very skillful with his hands to could build anything that he put his mind too. I'm sure that growing up on a New England farm during the depression had a lot to do with the do it yourself ingenuity.

We put down a concrete slab, built up the walls and then for the roof we took beams and wood recovered from a silo on the old Hawthorne Farms in Hillsboro Oregon. Today in this location is a large Intel facility named after the farm. Then came Electrical, plumbing, insulation, windows, and assorted other odds and ends.

The last thing to be done was linoleum over the concrete floor. We measured and cut pieces of the linoleum from the large roll. Each piece was carried into the house where glue was applied to the concrete then linoleum placed over the glue.

We were down to the last piece near the double door entry that gave access to the rest of the house when I heard a scrabble of claws. This sound was followed by a kitten at full speed crossing the smooth floor of the kitchen followed by her playmate. There was no possibility of either coming to a stop. The kittens, oblivious to their dilemma continued at perilous velocity.

Helpless from where I stood on the far side of the glue, I first saw Candy followed by Cocoa sail over the top of Dad who was on his hands and knees applying glue and into white and still very slippery glue. They cart wheeled, whirled about and performed in place kitty burn-outs as they attempted to gain traction. Dad muttered devastating words. I place my hands over my ears as he attempted to get a hold of each kitten in turn only to have the slide away. In desperation he pinned Candy to the floor. In desperation he through Candy to me, I side stepped proving myself to be an intelligent young boy avoiding the sharp talons.

Dad was not happy with me.

Eventually the kittens were captured and the kind person that my father was he immediately headed for the laundry sink. Both cats were quickly washed in soap and water to remove the glue. I'm sure some of glue came off but over the grumbling of my father I couldn't really be sure. Have you ever tried to bath a cat?

Without turning his head he shouted for lacquer thinner, the handyman's secret weapon. The not so secret weapon failed to noticeably remove the now thoroughly dried glue. After an additional soapy bath, Dad sighed with resignation.

For the next few weeks I had to put up with friends asking what sort of weird pets we had. The fur mostly stuck straight out and contained globs of white stuff dried to a rock hard consistency. I found myself constantly trying to pick chunks from the fur.

Eventually it wore off. But for months after I found clumps of old glue that I would carefully clipped free causing Candy and Cocoa to take on a motley appearance.

CHAPTER 17

Missy and the kittens

Missy came into my life as a replacement. My first kitten at 3 months old passed away while under the care of a vet. This was my first real pet after successfully raising guppies, that passing of my first kitten left me distraught and sure that in some way I was the cause of her death. I was very sad and found it difficult to smile. I passed the time going between home and school; nothing seemed to matter to my young mind.

One day after school on my way home I took a wide detour to stop at the pet store in down town Hillsboro. They rarely had cats or dogs, generally specializing in fish. This is where I obtained my guppies. The clerk nodded at me as I entered and went back to cleaning a tank. I was a familiar face in a relatively small quiet town.

I wondered along the bank of fish tanks admiring all of the brightly colored fish tanks. The Neon Tetra's flashing back and forth in there tank. As I reached the end of the fish tanks I saw movement in a wire cage further ahead of me. I stepped to the cage and peeked between the bars of the cage where I saw prettiest 6 week old blue point Siamese kitten. "When born young blue points are mostly white with steel grey ears, paws and tail." I sat on the floor and stuck my fingers through the cage opening trying to reach her, she played with my finger and lovingly rubbed her cheeks against me. It was love at first site, for the first time since the death of my kitten I felt joy at the touch of another kitten. We had only just met but when I called her she looked me in the eye and instantly melted my heart with her deep blue eyes.

I absolutely had to have her. I went to the clerk and told him please don't sell her I will be right back with my mother. He smiled and told me not to worry, I did any way. I rushed quickly out the door.

Mom worked in the law office across the street from the court house. That day it was a 2 block run. I anxiously threw the door open and raced into the office. I knew better then to start talking but was beside myself with impatience. Mom noticed me and called me by name but then went back to talking with the attorney. I remained quiet but danced if in urgent need of the little boys room. Mom picked up her purse and came around the partition and asked if I wanted to go next door to the Jinx café for an RC. I nodded my head while absolutely bursting with the news.

While sitting at the counter sipping my RC I ask Mom if I could have another kitten since mine had died. She felt that would be fine, so I asked if we could go up to the pet store right now? She was surprised at my excitement as I told her about the most beautiful little kitten.

True to her word we were soon leaving the pet store with my new blue point Siamese kitten nestled in my arms purring loudly. She spun like a top making sure I was stoking her back and next her tummy. I held her close thinking she will spin loose but she had no intention of leaving me.

Missy was my friend and constant companion, we watched TV together and slept together. If was home she was with me seeking love and affection. That first night she wanted to be in bed with me and not in her box. She was so small I was afraid I might roll over in bed injuring her. The mewing was insistent until I remove the cover of the box. She quickly climbed the bed cover purring deeply, I had held her in the crook of my arm until we both fell asleep. There was no doubt, we bonded and would always be close companions until her death many years later.

Siamese are very vocal cats; Missy was no exception and took every opportunity to let her wants be known. Additionally she was very social, any port in a storm would have been her motto or more correctly any lap will due as long as petting is involved. She loved to be near people and was not to be left out of any conversation. She was also very much a climber and would climb the drapes to sit or lay upon the supporting rod overhead.

Missy got along well with my brothers kitten that was a few months older, her name was Candy. Candy was also a Siamese but a seal point (White fur with dark chocolate brown points). Their favorite sleeping spot was on top of the old console TV. The large tube in the TV generated a generous amount of heat that warmed the top of the wood cabinet.

The first Christmas for the kittens was an adventure. They loved the wrapping paper chasing each other through the tunnels of colorful paper or just flat plowing into the piles of paper at full speed. They especially loved the new climbing post witch was otherwise referred to at the Christmas tree.

The first meeting of cat versus Christmas tree occurred as the cats were chasing each other through the house. They would run full tilt seeming to dodge every obstacle, in reality there were occasional collisions with walls and table legs. This was followed by a long pause at the cat would sit back and regain there wits. On this occasion they had reached top speed as they crossed the dining room and streaked across the living room floor headed for the Christmas tree. The tree decorated with glass balls and tinsel became there target as the lead cat leaped into the branches with the other close on her tail. They raced each other to the top of the seven foot tall tree reaching the top in a split second. Then from the top they launched themselves back toward the middle of the living room floor still in full chase mode. The tree shook and divested itself of several ornaments and slowly fell to the floor.

Dad said not a word. For a man full of cuss words and subject to sudden tempers made this a miracle in of its self. He left the room as we looked each other waiting for the shoe to drop. He soon returned from the garage with a swag hook and fishing line. The swag hook with a threaded end was turned into an overhead beam, the fishing line was tied to the top of the tree and hung from the hook. Stepping back Dad said his first word about the incident "there, that should take care of that".

My brother and I were Boy Scouts studying to complete our merit badges so that we could gain the next rank. At that time a scout started as a Tenderfoot and worked their way up to First Class Scout. These early ranks were gained by completing a list of activities from the Boy Scout Manual. Activities involved such items as camping, hiking and memorizing the Scout Laws, after the first three ranks came, Star, Life and then Eagle Scout. Part of ran was earning merit badges, each of the merit badges demonstrated advanced skills in a wide variety of areas. After obtaining 21 or more merit badges that included some that were required, you were eligible to complete your final tasks to become and Eagle Scout.

Missy participated in my pets merit badge. When she was the correct age I breed her with a pure breed male seal point Siamese. After becoming pregnant she was extra needy requiring extra care and attention. In preparation for the big day placed a box in my closet where it was safe and dark for the new kittens. I also added a large soft fluffy towel in the bottom of the box. This meant she would be near me and be reassured that everything would be safe.

My brother pursued his pets merit badge at the same time breeding his cat Candy. This also meant that the kittens would all be born near the same time.

One very early morning Missy woke me with frantic meows. I drug myself from bed slipping on my robe and slippers. Once prepared I followed her down the steps leading to the laundry room. Missy quickly slipped to the bottom of the steps her meows hardly missing a beat. I stumbled down the stair nearly stepping on something on the stairs. To my first surprise I found a new born kitten. I picked it up carefully and held it close to my chest to keep it warm.

Progressing through the laundry room I found my next little white bundled huddled on the cold floor. I added this kitten to the first cupping the small bundles carefully in my hands to keep them warm. Both kittens were all white without a sign of the Siamese markings.

Moving on towards the kitchen where I could hear Missy still frantic, I found another kitten on the kitchen floor. I cast about each room looking for more kittens as Missy followed me becoming more frantic by the moment. Fortunately there were no other foundlings, so I headed back upstairs to my bedroom and the carefully prepared but unused box.

When we reached the closet I wondered what to do, would Missy care for the kittens? I decided to risk placing the kittens in the box hoping it wasn't to cold. Missy hopped into the box as if nothing unusual had occurred, nestling down and licking each of the new born kittens. I watched for a while and then moved away to give her time with her pride, but she jumped from the box to follow me. So back to the box we went. It took a few days but eventually she would stay with the kittens. I'm sure I sighed with relief as she became a very attentive mother. Near the same time Candy had kittens but without the drama of dropping them like the Easter Bunny delivers eggs.

As the kittens eyes opened and they began to walk we started looking for homes. There was a high demand for Siamese cats and we had no trouble selling the kittens to good homes. Indeed it seems we were short on kittens.

To meet the demand for kittens we breed both cats again with better luck as Missy knew what to do. One night after reading late I laid down my book and turned off my light to sleep. Missy as usual lay at my side contented and bulging with kittens.

Sometime in the early morning I awoke unsure of what had woken me. I could hear Missy purring and soon realized she was under the covers between my knees. Unusual as she didn't like sleeping under the covers. Lifting the covers I first saw Missy's bright blue eyes and then 5 little kittens all nestled warm between my knees. Well I thought, this is better than finding them strewn about the house.

I admired the kittens for a bit but then realized I need to take care of my own business. Lifting my leg to ease out of bed I caught the soft flesh of my inner thigh on a set of new kitten claws. Yes, new born kittens have claws and they are a sharp as a hypodermic needle. Adding to this I had four out of these sharp claws imbedded in my flesh. I stifled a scream and carefully lowered my leg so that I could disengage the kitten from my leg.

The box in the closet was just the right size. Missy could curl up in the box and just have room for the 5 kittens to nurse. The box appeared to be brimming with fur. Not to be upstaged, Candy delivered three beautiful kittens again with little drama or fanfare.

This time around included an unfortunate event, Candy came into heat when her kittens were three days old. The poor thing was incapable of taking care of the kittens though she did give it a valiant try. We started feeding the kittens by hand and doing our best to keep them warm. This was very difficult, requiring they be feed every 2-3 hours. We were tired that first night and fell asleep in the early morning hours.

The next morning there was a miracle. During the night Missy had transferred all of Candy's kittens to her own box. When we found the three kittens in the now overflowing box my thoughts went to Missy wondering where she might be. At this point there was a meow and I saw the Missy was also in the box with only her head sticking above a sea of kittens she was nursing.

I hunted up a larger box and prepared it. The kittens were then moved to this box. Missy then moved each kitten back into the smaller box where she raised all of the kittens.

We left one night for an overnight at the beach. While we were gone our kind neighbor Mr. Holt watched the house, cats and kittens. He always acted though he didn't care about the cats but one day I caught him with all three in his lap. He was talking to them as they enjoyed his attention.

Returning from the beach on Sunday we found a large banner across the front of our house. "Forest Street Cat O' factory". Mr. Holt and my mother played jokes back and forth for years and this was just one more in a long line of incidents.

We made this the last of the kittens. The last remaining kitten without a home captured Mom's heart so we were now a three Siamese cat home.

CHAPTER 18

Mr. West

Mr. West was a great man in my life, he was of strong character, firm resolution and gentle nature. He was a man that other men looked up to and hoped to be. Born in 1916 he grew up in an earlier age those of the great generation who then served in US Army of World War II. He saw action in Europe but rarely if ever spoke of it. He came back home and married his high school sweet heart. Together they raised five girls in there Hillsboro Oregon home as well as dozens of boys that were part of Boy Scout troop 538.

Mister West was our Boy Scout Scoutmaster. He was the one who guided us in our activities and helped us grow to be the men we are today. Mr West was employed by Portland General Electric as a lineman climbing electrical poles and seeing that the citizens of Hillsboro had consistent access to electrical power.

I joined cub scouts earning the top rank of Lion when the award was then replaced by creation of Webelos. Webelos was made up of older cub scouts preparing to move into the Boy Scouts. We still joined in with the Cub Scout Pack but had activities more in spirit with what we would later be part of in Boy Scouts.

My father took me to my first Boy Scout troop meeting when I turned 11. There I met Mr. West, a balding, white haired gentleman more than six feet tall and deeply tanned. He was toughness and sinew though slightly stocky he did not carry any excess baggage on his frame.

A call went out and the other Boy Scouts filed in with the American flag with 48 stars, it was over 10 years since the 50th state had joined the union but the flag was still honored as it had been donated to the troop by a widow whose husband had died in World War II. The boys also brought in the white and red flag of the troop with their awards draped over the ball on the top.

Everyone stood at attention and saluted the American flag while repeating the pledge of allegiance. All done very solemn and respectfully. Afterwards Mr. West introduced me to the troop. The Senior Patrol leader Steve was 17 but looked much older. I listened as he assigned me to the Jaguar patrol.

We broke up into patrols and moved to separate rooms in the church to work on scout activities. The jaguar patrol was working on their Morse code. They setup and Morse code sender and receiver. Then the Patrol leader tapped out a message as we listened and wrote down the message. I was lost in the maze of dashes and dots but the other scouts helped me through until the Steve collected me and we went back to troop room.

That night Steve quizzed me on my requirements for Tenderfoot badge and signed off on three requirements. Over the next two weeks Mr. West tested me on knowledge of the uniform, badge, sign, motto, law and oath signing off on each as they were completed. On the fourth week I received my first badge of rank, Tenderfoot.

The next rank was second class, but as it included more complicated items such as three separate three mile hikes, trailing, stalking, tracking, learning map and compass it took another year.

After earning my Tenderfoot rank Steve announced the next hike. We would be going into the Mount Hood wilderness area on the Burnt Creek trail. We broke into patrols to discuss the hike. Our Patrol leader Jim said we should have a meeting at his house on Saturday and bring our gear.

Dad had taken us on hikes and camping but never an overnight back packing trip. So Dad took me to the Wigwam store where we picked out an inexpensive canvas back pack with an aluminum frame. We looked at everything else and picked out a aluminum mess kit and canteen. We looked over the tents but they were all either very expensive or heavy canvas affairs.

Dad removed and old piece of plastic from the garage and we called it my ground cloth and tent. Along with a ball of twine and a couple of sticks I could build my own tent. The plastic sheet went into the pack with my clean underwear, mess kit, utensils and sleeping bag. A very basic kit missing such things a matched and food.

At the patrol meeting we discovered that only three of us were going so Jim called the other patrols and we combined our food purchase as there were only going to be 8 of us going. Jim glanced in my pack and made a couple of suggestions that I added to my gear.

Saturday morning early we all arrived at the church where our scout meetings were held. Mr. West arrived in his 1964 white Chevrolet truck and camper shell. We didn't take any other vehicles so with three people in the front, 5 boys in the camper with all the gear we headed out highway 26 east towards Mount Hood.

The trip was over two hours and the day grew warm. Some of the boys had brought sodas and candy bars that they munch on. It was relief that we pulled into the Burnt Lake trail head parking lot. We jumped from the truck and stretched our cramped muscles. We looked up to see Mount Hood towering over the parking lot, a rushing stream ran by and a few trees. A trail led off gently up hill and soon turned into the trees.

Mount Hood is the last mountain in the Cascade range located in Oregon. The Cascade range runs through Oregon and Washington with several snowcapped volcanic peaks. This 11,249 ft (3429 m) peak last erupted in 1866.

Pulling our packs from the back of the pickup little did we know what lay ahead. Being the youngest of the bunch I stuck close to Mr. West while the older boys tossed on there packs and charged up the trail at nearly a run. The trail was very quiet that day and we didn't encounter any other people during the weekend.

Mr. West indicated that I should go ahead of him so we headed up the trail in the dust left by the other Scouts who were now out of sight. It wasn't long before the switch backs started. These still are some of the steepest I have every hiked.

We soon came upon the other boys, they were collapsed and breathing hard laying on there sides and backs with packs still attached. It was now a sorry group of red face exhausted boys. Mr. West stopped and pulled out his snack bag. He called it bird seed and passed it around. He had made up his own combination of peanuts, walnuts, almonds, pretzels, gum drops and M&M candies. We each took a handful grateful for the snack.

Eventually after a rest we continued on our 6.6 mile hike witch continued to run through fir trees but now only gentle gained elevation. The boys were all quieter now and we stayed together as we reached a beautiful clear lake with the reflection of Mount Hood covered with snow standing above. It was a welcome relief for the day was quite warm.

We spent the afternoon first swimming and then exploring. We enjoyed the cool water and spread out to enjoy our personal space. Mr. West joined us and took a quick plunge in to the cool waters.

Some of us hiked to the top of a small hill above the lake to be treated to a dramatic view of Mount Hood and the reflection of Mount Hood in the still waters of Burnt Lake. It was just us the lake the trees and Mount Hood.

After the swim we took a hike up a small treeless knob near the lake where some of the boys with there camera's took pictures of Mount Hood and its reflection in the lake.

Later back a camp I had my first lesson on how to cook over and open fire. Back packing stoves were rare and even non-existent at the time so if you took over night hikes you cooked over a fire. We built up the fire and then let it burn down to coals. Coals are best as you can control the heat better. One of the older boys had carried a heavy cast iron skillet. This is not typical camp gear but a great tool for cooking over and open fire.

While I have no idea what we had for dinner we ate well and were satisfied. When all the dishes had been cleaned we gathered around the fire to talk about the day. Jim brought out a bag of marshmallows which brought on a scramble into the nearby bushes to cut and sharpen our sticks for roasting. That Night Mr. West talked about his service in the military and later in World War II. He had fought in the battle fields of France facing gun fire so that others might have freedom. This gentle reverent man heaved I sigh and gave thanks to God for returning him home safe again. This was the only time he spoke of his service in such detail.

I had setup my piece of plastic propping up each end and leaving a fold as a ground cover to lay my sleeping bag. I had closed off both ends for privicay and may surely of suficated that night but fore Mr. West's intervention. Mr. West was opened holes at the front and back so that I would have a nice flow of air through my shelter. I listened to the two older boys who had carried in the heavy cast iron skillet as they complained and groaned over there blisters. From the level of noise emanating from their tent they must have been the largest blisters on record. I didn't have boots for my first hike so I had warn my converse high tops and not suffered a blister. Then with the gentle hum of the insects and the occasional splash of a fish I drifted off to sleep.

The hike back the next day was much quieter without the wild charge up the hill the previous day. We were all very quiet in the back of the pickup yet completely satisfied with the energy we had expended. As I drifted off to sleep my thoughts were on the next adventure we would be taking.

We made many trips camping and back packing over the years with Mr. West. He was always available and happy to take responsibility for our health and wellbeing. His five daughters eventually each married but didn't interrupt our scouting functions. One of the local administrators named Serge took notice over the years and entered Mr. West's name for the Silver Beaver Award.

The Silver Beaver Award was created in 1931 to recognize adult leaders who have had an impact in the lives of young boys. The award is made to those who do not seek recognition but earn it through there selfless service.

Serge arranged the award ceremony so that Mr. West would be clueless as to what was occurring. His wife and my parents were all in on the surprise. The story developed that my brother and I were selected as the honor guard and flag presenters for the Scouting Awards event to be held in the Civic Auditorium in Portland Oregon.

On the night of the presentation Mr. and Mrs. West picked up my brother, Mother, father and I at our home driving his 1964 Dodge 880 Wagon. I had always been fascinated by this car as it had a manual transmission but you pushed buttons on the dash to shift the gears. I sat in front between Mr. and Mrs. West as we headed out of town. During the ride Mr. West stopped to pickup a piece of sheet rock that had fallen in the road. The sheet rock still head nails sticking out. Upon returning to the car he grinned at me and said "I did my good deed for the day". It was an appropriate action, befitting the purpose of our trip. He would soon learn how fitting his comment would be for this evening's event.

We arrived at the Civic Auditorium and while my brother and I were escorted back stage the others found seats in the audience. The placed was full with nearly everyone of the 3000 seats occupied. My brother and I were first on the stage carrying the American and Oregon flags as the audience rose and sang the national anthem. Afterwards the Scout Oath and Law were repeated by Scouts and adult leaders in the crowd. The presenter next took the stand and spoke long and eloquently about Scouting and the Silver Beaver Award.

Finally the time came for the awards. My brother and I still stood on the stage in full uniform and had a firsthand view of all that was occurring. The announcer called John W. West of troop 538. At the same time the spot light moved across the audience until it shone from Mr. West's bald pate. He looked back and forth wondering who they were calling, this humble man never for a moment thought he would be the one they were searching for. With a nudge Mrs. West told him to stand up and with a blush and smile he stood and made his way to the stage. On the stage Serge gave a long speech on this man who had unselfishly dedicated his life to helping boys become better men and citizens. Serge drew out the award on its blue and white ribbon and while he placed it about his neck camera's flashed and the audience let loose with thunderous applause.

After the ceremony we gather around Mr. West and congratulated him. But soon his attention centered on my brother and I, he asked the question foremost on his mind. "Did you boys know about this?"

Mr. West rarely wore his Silver Beaver Award but on the occasion of my Eagle Scout Award ceremony he made an exception and wore it with his full uniform.

Mr. West was the greatest man I ever knew. I stand here today and can say that if it had not been for him I would not be the man I 'am today. My only regret was that I was unable to spend more time with him before his death in 1997 at the age of 81.

John W. West

Born April 22, 1915

Died March 27, 1997 (Age 81)

**Married June 12, 1946 Yellowstone
Montana to Lois Bauer Nugent**

Father: S.M. West

CHAPTER 19

My Best Friend Kenny

Over the years I have made a lot of friends and lost track of many, some may say lost but truly no friend is lost only misplaced. While growing up I had many friends coming in and out of my life but one that stuck around for decades was Kenny. We met in 7th grade and would spend decades as friends never quite loosing track of each other.

Our first meeting occurred in the Poynter Junior High cafeteria. The room was arranged using long tables butted end for end. Each day I would eat my lunch with some people that I knew through long association, that is we had started kindergarten together. One day a new kid (Kenny) showed up and sat with us each day. We didn't really talk much and he looked really young for 7th grade, at first I thought he must be a fifth grader.

During the first week after Kenny had joined our group and while we were sitting together eating lunch, the janitor approached with a bucket. Upon reaching the table the janitor produced a stick and used it to fish around in the bucket. The smell was unpleasant and I promptly lost interest in my lunch. Finding what he wanted the janitor drew out a red coat and looked at Kenny. "Found it in the toilet, do you want it?" Kenny looked up and as politely as possible replied "no thank you". I was repulsed by the fact the janitor brought something into the cafeteria from a toilet but curious as to the story behind it. Kenny soon related the story of how he had been harassed by some boys ever since he started school. He fought back but was too small and outnumbered. That morning they had taken his coat when they ran off.

From that day forward I joined up with Kenny and we spent quite a bit of time together. I was part of the wrestling team and had been wrestling since I was in 4th grade. Most of the bullies respected that and left Kenny alone. There was one big fellow that wouldn't let it go and constantly threatened the both of us. I ignored him as each day he would repeat his mantra "Meet behind the school, if you're not chicken". This go to be really annoying as he would follow us to class yelling and shouting. I had nothing to prove so I just kept ignoring him.

We avoided the big bull for as long as we could but one day the encounter finally became inevitable. As we were leaving the front door of the school he approached and let me know it was now or never. He charged wind milling his arms. I dropped one foot back then bringing my fist up from my side sunk it into his stomach sinking into the generous roll of fat. He dropped like a stone and began groaning while he held his stomach. I was totally unprepared and stood staring down at the bully that was 5 inches taller and at least 50 pounds heavier than myself.

The bully's bad day was about to get worse as he had unfortunately selected to confront me in front of Superintendent Stuarts office window. Mr. Stuart knew he was a problem and had been trying to catch him. Mr. Stuart asked what had happened and I told him, he let Kenny and

I leave while the bully was escorted to the office for some much needed disciplinary action.

That afternoon Kenny invited me to his home for the first time where I met his mother Betty. They lived at the far South end of 5th street and a beautiful if run down historic house overlooking Jackson bottom. Betty fed us homemade soup and fresh bread, and then we sat and talked for an hour like two adults. She was not at all like my mother, she drank beer and smoked but even with those faults I grew to love her.

It wasn't long before summer arrived and Kenny and I were getting around town on our bikes. We stopped at the hobby shop where there was a brand new metal detector on sale. Kenny told me how we could make big Kenny's finding lost coins and gold jewelry. Kenny readily spent his savings to purchase one and after he found a few coins I dug out my hard earned money and purchased the same brand. These were very basic with a loop to run over the ground attached to a box by a 3 foot rod.

Within two weeks Kenny found a cigar box of coins buried near the front gate of an abandon home over on 6th street. It was a great find, many of the coins were quite old and worth more than face value. I continued to search with the detector all throughout the summer but the best I found was a roll of pennies in some tall grass at the Washington county fairgrounds.

We ended that summer with a camping adventure. We were fortunate to have a Boy Scout Camp ground named Camp Ireland North of Hillsboro. The previous year my Boy Scout Troop had a weekend trip where we honed our outdoor skills. Over the years I was involved in dozens of improvement projects but in 1970 the camp was very basic. McKay creek ran through the property but there was no bridge across like there is today.

We loaded up our bikes with a tent, sleeping bags, food and other essentials and peddled our way to the camp. As we passed the entrance the caretaker waved at us. Kenny and I with our two little brothers wandered around looking at the selection of camp sites but Kenny was not satisfied. He wanted something more isolated. Soon one of the younger brothers found a log across the McKay creek so we stashed our bikes in the brush and crossed the creek to the other side.

The other side of the creek was isolated and included a small clearing where we setup our tent. The tent was really only a two person affair but all four of us tossed our sleeping bags into the tent and setup about building a fire for our dinner.

Over dinner we sat around the fire telling stories and talking but we were all quite exhausted. We each made our way into the tent and did not notice the cramped quarters. We slept deeply and did not awaken until the sun had already crept up the next morning. At that point there was an urgent exodus accompanied by sharp exclamations as we climbed over each other still in our sleeping bags. Sighs of relief filled out camp site as we each found our own bush.

That day we explored the clearing and the woods. At the far end there was an old fence that was fallen down and had seen better days. The next year our Boy Scout troop would be back out to replace the fence and start improvements to the area that included a shelter.

We had lots of fun and fresh air. I'm sure that's what led us to believing we could pretend we were Indians (Native Americans) living in the wilderness like my ancestors. We really had very little idea of how they lived but we all skinned down to our undershorts and pretended they were native garb. We then crept through the forest in our bare feet where we cut sticks and practiced throwing them like spears.

That night we sat around the fire again dressed but feet still bare as we pulled out thorns and stickers from our tender areas. We also told ghost stories that night with each scaring us a bit more than the last. We soon had worked ourselves up to the point where we all sought shelter together in the tent.

I awoke in the middle of the night when Kenny poked me in the ribs. I remained still as I often did as he whispered, there's someone out there. I could hear footsteps and then the sound of someone dragging there knife across our rain fly. We knew that something had to be done and that our younger siblings needed to be protected or our parents would never let us back into the house.

We laid quiet in the darkness letting our fear and determination build. Then we burst from the tent door intent on getting to our spears and discouraging our attackers. Kenny's brother raised his head with a what! As I put my foot into his stomach for my leap from the door departing with the sound of his oof.

I had a good start but was almost immediately had as one of the strangers in front of me. I ducked to the side and rolled but she turned towards me and said mooooo! Sanity quickly returned as I realized our attackers was a small herd of cows that had entered through the broken down fence.

In the silence that followed I heard Kenny's brother gasping for breath and my own brother making loud exclamations in the dark. I could see Kenny with his spear standing on the other side of the tent. He looked at me and raised his shoulders as he lifted his hands up.

After day break we left the cows behind, returned to our bikes. On the ride home we swore to never tell another ghost story while camping.

CHAPTER 20

Wilson River

Highway 26, also known as the Sunset Highway is the highway that leads straight to the Pacific Ocean. Leaving Portland Oregon as a divided six lane freeway continues west as first a divided four lane free then finally reaching the town of Banks Oregon becomes two lane highway six that winds its way through the Oregon Coast Range until reaching highway 101 on the Oregon coast.

Near Banks Oregon the Highway splits, 26 continues on a Northerly route ending at highway 101 near Seaside Oregon. The Southerly route continues as Highway Six also known as the Wilson River Highway. The Wilson River route is much more scenic as it winds through the country side and up in to the Coast Ranges. Near the top of the pass it's joined in its journey to the Ocean by the Wilson River. Near Tillamook Oregon on the coast the mountain ridges end quite suddenly with the open dairy pastures that provide the milk for the Tillamook Cheese Factory.

The Wilson River was our backyard and the scene for many of our summer adventures. Near the top of the pass the Wilson River starts small but quickly grows as other streams and springs join in the run to the ocean. The rocky bottom and fish can be seen in the clear water, the banks are covered by boulders and rocky outcroppings that add to the character of the river. The deep pools reach up to 60 feet deep as it flows through its narrow channel between steep sloping ridges. The river remains narrow for much of its journey but as it reaches the Tillamook basin it widens to nearly a mile at the Pacific Ocean.

We had visited the river with our parents for picnics and a dip in the cool water during the warm summer months. The summer after receiving my driver's license gave us the freedom to explore several miles of the river. Our adventure started in June after berry picking completed. It was one of those hot sticky mornings that we decided it was time to cool off.

Kenny and I jumped in my old Chevy and headed out to find cooler weather. We ended up on the Wilson River highway and soon looking down on the Wilson River. The bank to the river was a steep rocky slope whose loose dirt and rock made it difficult to reach the river. Stripped to our cut offs and sandals we slipped and slid our way down the slope to the river.

The river was too shallow for a swim at this point so in search of deeper water we struggled back up the slope to the car. We headed farther West until we came to a wide turn out. A quick look told us this was the place we were looking for. We made our way down the embankment where it leveled out somewhat into a rock shelf. At the river the rocky shelf dropped off into a deep pool, the 6 foot drop appeared to offer plenty of hand holds to climb back up. We kicked off our sandals and with no thought for rocks jumped from the ledge into the cold water. As I came up cooler and sputtering, I had forgot that the stream had been fed by snow melt up until early May and the water was still quite brisk. With quick strokes I made it back to the bank the up the rock wall to where Kenny stood shivering and wet.

We spent the rest of the day exploring the next few miles of the river making plans for a bigger adventure. When we felt the need to cool off we took quick dips in the cold water.

The next weekend we came to camp bringing our inner tubes, scuba masks and snorkels. We camped along the shore at the first rock shelf. We had a small fire to warm up as the sun went down. On a dare the Kenny, myself and our brothers jumped from the cliff into the cold water. Afterwards we stretched out in our sleeping bags, finding a comfortable rock and did our best to sleep through the night. Sleep was not difficult for young bodies and we awoke the next morning hungry and with no food, a failure in our planning. I drove into Tillamook to pick up some food. Upon my return I found everyone excited by there latest find. A deep hole in the river where they had been diving I put on my mask and joined in exploring the hole witch had to be nearly 30 feet deep.

On Monday morning I returned to my job at Scotty's Auto body where I was assisting the painter sanding down cars. Not a very exciting job not to say hot and dusty. By the time the weekend came back I was excited to head back to the river. I only worked here for another month before they shut down. I was actually relieved as I hadn't partial to the work.

That weekend found the four of us back on the Wilson River in a canoe. We dropped in the same place we had been swimming the previous weekend. We drifted down the river, rowed when needed and carried the canoe over shallow stretches when we needed. We saw pretty girls occasionally sitting along the bank.

We swung wide around a broad corner of the river and spied a rope hanging from a branch over the river. We put into shore where we took turns swinging out over the water and dropping from the rope. We were having great fun until swinging over the water laughing I forgot to drop into the water. Swinging back to the shore I thought to myself I will just swing up and drop back in where I had launched from. What I forgot was that I was barefoot and the shore was rough stone. Swinging over the shore my foot slammed into a rock and I dropped limply to the rocks grasping my foot and moaning in agony. Surely my foot was broken and I saw the rest of my summer fade. At the same time I dropped I heard everyone yell at me because I let go of the rope. I'm certain I didn't care as I peered at them through a fog of pain.

Everyone else continued to take turns on the rope as I sat with my foot in the cold water to ease the pain and swelling. Soon we were back in the canoe paddling down the river witch was now deep enough that we didn't have to lift it over rocks.

When the sun started going down we put into the shore where Kenny made his way back to the highway. We had come much further than he expected, so when a couple stopped to ask if he wanted a ride it was quickly accepted. We hadn't learned at that time the risks of hitch-hiking, which was yet to come.

We spent the remainder of the summer weekends on the Wilson River. The group of boys growing until there were over a dozen. Near the end of August we were back down to the river but with our parents and had a big picnic. We even took turns jumping from High Bridge into the water below. Our parents from different back grounds all seemed to get along well.

Dad had painted up some old parts with bright orange paint and tossed them into the river. Whenever one of us brought it up he would pay us a quarter. On one toss he hit one of the really deep pools that had to go over 30 feet deep. Try as we might there was no reaching it. Dad came to me and said if I retrieved it he would give me five dollars. I know he was thinking he didn't want to leave garbage in the river.

I dove in and swam as hard as I could knowing speed was my only ally and wishing I had my swim fins. Soon my lungs were bursting but I had reached the part. I grasped the part and swam for the surface the air in my lungs already exhausted. It seemed like a lot longer up then down and as my vision was blurring and I thought I would black out I reached the surface where I took in great lungful's of air. At first I was to tired to swim to shore but eventually slowly swam back to where Dad was waiting with my five dollars. I was cold even though the day was hot and with the bill grasped in my hand went back to the car where huddle in the back seat wrapped up in blankets.

We enjoyed time on the river for a few years but nothing compared to that first year. The best part was exploring and once we had been over that ground it was old news. With the start of school that fall and the cooler weather we quickly forgot our summer adventure and looked forward to the next holiday from school.

CHAPTER 21

First Beach Trip

During spring break of 1975 before starting my final year of high school at Hillsboro Hilhi. My friend Kenny and I became part of an escapade known at the beach trip. Behind our backs I'm sure it was known as the disaster weekend.

My close friend Kenny owned a blue 1969 Pontiac Lemans with, black interior. The car was fast, really too fast for a teenager. It was a car that his father who was a professional gambler picked up in a three day card game. Being the father of a professional gambler had its ups and downs but mostly downs. When Kenny's father came home from one of these gambling marathons he would be very tired and immediately hit the hay. This was the signal for his Mother to sneak in and remove folding money from his jeans. You should know this had nothing to do with deep ulterior motives, it was merely the means that she had developed over the years to make sure the bills were paid and that there would be grocery money.

Kenny suggested on Thursday night that we should make an overnight trip in the Pontiac to visit the Pacific Ocean. We lived an hour from the beach so this would not really be a trip far from home but it meant that we could be on our own and do as we pleased. After getting permission from our parents we planned the trip. We would start from Forest Grove and headed to Lincoln City on the Southern Oregon coast. The trip would take us through Gaston, McMinnville and Sheridan.

The range of mountains between the Willamette Valley and the Pacific Ocean is called the Coast Range it made up of forest land, and national forests such as Tillamook and Clatsop. The highest peak is Mary's Peak at 4101 feet. Our journey would over Highway 18 would mean going no higher than a 1000 feet elevation.

On Friday Kenny swung by my house where I through in a bag of clouths, sleeping bag and back packing tent. Food was a second thought but I tossed in a couple of snacks. The real treasure was the $100 bill that Kenny's Dad had provided. We were to use it for whatever we might need. At that time there were no ATM machines or cash cards, many people didn't even have a credit card and especially not a 17 year old. It was a good thing that Kenny's Dad had the perspective to do our thinking for us.

Along the way stopped in Sheridan Oregon and visited with my Uncle Hugh at his hardware store. They had come out from Vermont and purchased Ivy Hardware store in Sheridan. They renamed it Fitzgerald's Hardware store and operated it for many years. This was one of the old timey hardware stores where you could find most anything you wanted if you had the time and patience. Kenny wandered the isles as I talk with my uncle. When it came time to go I had a difficult time getting Kenny to go. He's the sort that has to look at each and every item in a store before he feels free to leave.

We passed through the Van Duzer Corridor state scenic section of highway 18 eventually passing through the town of Otis then Lincoln City. I stared at the Pixie Kitchen as we passed through town and as we reached the D river we had our first good view of the Pacific Ocean. It had been raining so that everything was still wet and the clouds hung heavily out over the ocean.

When we passed through Nelscott I remembered that my Scout Master John West had his beach house here. I had spent many memorable nights there with my family and with the Boy Scout troop leadership team. During one trip there with the Boy Scouts in addition to Mister West my father went along as the Assistant Scout Master. The weekend was stormy and the waves beat up against the sea wall. Between Mister West's house the ocean was a narrow street and a row of houses, the row of houses set back a short distance from the sea wall.

As the wind increased and the water churned it created great foamy maps of sea foam. Mister West and I watched as the elderly neighbor across the street came out the front door of her home using a walker. She then made her way along a walkway to the sea wall. We soon realized she was in trouble. When she reached the sea wall she did a snappy turn-about with the walker and dashed madly away. At this point a large mass of sea foam came over the wall and dropped upon her. We dashed down to help but she was fine other than being anxious to get back into her house.

That night we enjoyed a nice fire and while some of the boys played a game my father and I ventured out into the dark for a walk. We made our way down to a small public area where the sea wall jutted out with a viewing area above Nelscott Beach. To the right was a ramp leading down to the ocean which you could use to walk on the sand. But tonight the ocean with every few waves was washing against the sea wall. Dad and I ventured a short way down the ramp and looked out at the ocean. Dad suddenly raced down the ramp, I stood still astonished at his action. He scooted along the wet sand near the wall as I watched a large wave wash over him. When the water receded he was not to be seen. I called and called dashing down the ramp only to be chased back by the waves, I knew that Dad had to be in trouble. I turned and ran back to Mister West's house to get help. As I ran, I bumped into someone on the dark street. This person grabbed me and held fast. I soon realized it was my Dad, I was beyond relieved. I turned out that he had dashed up a steep stairwell that we couldn't see in the dark. Later as we dried off in the house I had to ask Dad why he had run down the beach. The answer to this mystery? He had thought there was a glass fishing float.

Eventually Kenny and I made it down to Agate beach a few miles North of Newport. If you have spent any time on the Oregon coast you will find the stores have many items of beautiful jewelry that contain highly polished agates. Our goal was to scour the beach for agates in hopes of making our own jewelry. Over the years we have collected several pounds but after a few feeble attempts determined that polishing the stones took an enormous effort not to speak of the skill required to create the settings. Today I'm no longer collector but enjoy admiring them.

When we reached Agate beach just north of Newport Oregon the weather was still cool but the sun was peaking between clouds and we were cheerful about our prospects. We parked along the highway 101 and dashed to down to the sand looking for agates. We had soon picked up several nice rocks and stuffed them into our pockets. Down on the beach it felt much warmer and I had grown hungry and thirsty. It was at this point I flagged Kenny down and let him know I was going into Newport. He decided to stay on the beach until I returned.

I hopped into the Pontiac and headed for the nearest grocery store. By the time I was exiting the store I was hungry beyond my teenage endurance. I sat in the car and had a bite before heading back, I no longer had any money left but knew Kenny had enough for the both of us.

Slid behind the wheel and swung the door closed, where I was rewarded with the clicking sound of a dead battery. Nothing happened; the engine didn't even turn over. This was nothing new for the Pontiac it occurred so frequently that we carried jumper cables in the car trunk. We spent hours up to this point tracking down and repairing electrical issues in the Pontiac but continued to have problems.

I started asking people coming out of the store if they would be willing to give me a jump but each shook their head. There was a business across the street, a gas station so I started asking people there. One fellow popped up and said sure he could help and stated that he would be over shortly.

A few minutes later he showed up in his Dodge pickup. It wasn't but a moment and I had the Pontiac started and the cables put away. The man then said that I should join him at the gas station across the street. An unusual request but I thought maybe he some idea what was wrong with the car. So I headed over to the gas station, something I wished I had never done. I parked the Pontiac in front of the station but left it running to make sure the battery charged.

The man who had provided the jump approached and handed me a bill for $50. I was stumped until he explained he was the station attendant and that was what they charged for a jump. I was appalled, I had no idea he worked at the station and the cost was ludicrous. This was the first time I had ever been charged for a jump. Well I had no money and it took a little dickering but I got him to hold the spare tire until I could return with the money.

From the perspective of several years, I would never put up with this today, he never stated there was a charge or that he worked for the station and therefore was attempting to defraud. As a 17 year old I lacked the perspective that I would acquire later and the membership in AAA.

I was not happy and very agitated as I hopped back in the Pontiac. I headed South out of Newport to retrieve our money and the spare tire. When I reached Agate beach Kenny was sitting on a rock next to the road wearing a hang dog expression on his face. "I lost it, it just floated out across the waves". I just looked at him perplexed not comprehending what he was telling me. This was his story; he had been collecting agates and stuffing them into his front jeans pocket for safe keeping. During one trip to the pocket his hand exited with the $100 dollar bill in tow, it broke free and with the help of the wind headed out over the waves. All our money was gone and so was my chance to get our tire back. Some might wonder at this event but then they would have to know Kenny. Some days bad luck followed him around like a hungry dog.

It was my turn to hang my head. I then related my story and we commiserated in silence.

Back on the road to Newport with Kenny driving we arrived back at the gas station. Kenny argued with the attendant for several minutes their voices rising to shoots but it did no good. During this time I sat in the car with the engine still running. It had not been turned off since the jump in the grocery parking lot.

We turned over option in our heads. Remember this was before ATM machines and cell phones so there was not to be a quick remedy. One thing we were sure of was that we would not call Kenny's Dad but would solve it ourselves.

We searched the car and our pockets for any spare money but that was no help. It was then that we remember we were members of the Masonic lodge youth organization DeMolay. We determined to take advantage of or Masonic Lodge ties so headed to the local lodge. We didn't expect anyone to be at the local Masonic Temple but found a list of contact numbers on the front door. From a pay phone using one of our last quarters we called the first number and spoke to the mason's spouse. She directed us to his business where we soon found ourselves in an unusual machine shop.

There were miles of copper wire and they were winding it onto coils that went to large electric motors. The shop was not to big but looked to have been a three bay automotive repair shop at one time. Kenny entered an office and spoke with the owner who was the mason about our problem and needs. It took some convincing but Kenny it good at that and he eventually loaned us the $50 dollars and accepted our IOU. Upon our return home we promptly mailed him the money. We were so grateful we never even thought of doing otherwise.

With money in hand we headed back out to the car witch we had turned off. Again it wouldn't start and we returned to the machine shop for assistance, which they did at no charge I might add. Back to the gas station where we left the Pontiac running, turned over the money and got our spare tire back from a different attendant. We jump in again and headed North towards Tillamook. The sun was slowly going down over the ocean and clouds were sweeping in from the North along with a drizzle of rain.

As we drove North the rain increased with the darkness making it difficult to see the road ahead with its well-worn lines. Highway 101 winds like a garden snake and moves up and down. At times you find your self at the top of a 200 foot cliff and then back down to sea level. It was through this murky darkness we made our way. The head lights of the Pontiac slowly dimmed as the battery started to fail. It was at this point we both had our windows open and heads hanging out to provide direction in gloom.

Soon ahead of us we spied the backend of a vehicle with several lights. As we drew near we determined it was a truck and camper moving no faster than ourselves. With great hope we speculated that they were headed somewhere to camp and that we ourselves could also find rest.

I spotted a sign as the camper turned onto a side road. I shined my flash light on the sign and it was welcomed news. Cape Lookout State park and Campground. What a relief, though the campground was still several miles ahead. Eventually the camper turned into the campground entrance with us close behind. The entrance booth was closed so we continued on looking for a site to park our weary bones. At this point what head lights we had did not help in our search and I hopped out of the car using my flash light to guide us down the aisles until I spotted an open spot.

Once parked, we sat in the idling car listening to the rain on the roof, then with fingers crossed turned the car off.

We pulled out the tent and had it up fairly quickly as I was experienced with setting up in the dark from my Boy Scout trips. While Kenny got our gear and sleeping bags into the tent I went looking for camp fire wood. I found wood left behind by a previous camper and by the time I got back to our site the rain had stopped.

The fire helped to warm us up but we were still hungry and snacked on the last of the crackers. But we had a surprise coming. The woman in the next camp site came over to let us know they had too much food and wondered if we were interested? After quietly thinking this over we quickly followed back to their site where we hungrily devoured every morsel offered. She was there with her husband and two small children stay in there camper. They were very kind, I remembered that kindness many years later when my wife and I helped out a pair of starving campers.

I slept well and as far as I know so did Kenny. In the morning we awoke to find the back end of the tent had collapsed and the bottom our sleeping bags wet from the nights rain. The tent had a single pole at the back that had a tendency to fall over. In this case I blamed it on Kenny's big feet. We were hungry again but with no breakfast waiting and we had another dilemma at our door step.

The park ranger came by as we were just getting up to collect the campsite funds. He saw we were just crawling out wet and tired so decided to come back. We started the search for money by going through all our pockets, this got us 75 cents of the two dollars we needed. Then back to the car and a more thorough search, this time pulling out the back seat we found 23 more cents. We were tapped out and desperate so Kenny started going to each camp site to borrow the needed funds. Again our kind campers helped us out and the ranger was soon paid.

The car was packed and it was time to start the car. We found a willing volunteer for a jump after we pushed the Pontiac back out into the roadway. Soon the car was started and we were on our way. The day was still cold but the sun came out to guide us on our way. It took little discussion but we decided to pack it in and head for home.

From the campground we passed through Tillamook and headed out highway 6. There was snow along the road and at the summit a couple of feet deep. We pulled off and hoped out of the car to have an impromptu snow ball fight in the warm sun. We then returned to the car spun the key and as the Pontiac roared to life pulled onto the road and completed our journey home.

Pulling into Kenny's driveway he turned the Pontiac off and turned to me with his quirky smile. "You know" he said, "After the snowball fight the car started up without a jump". I was thankful it did but still not very happy with its quirky attitude.

We went over to the appliance shop to talked with Kenny's Dad. He laughed a few times and when I got to the part about giving him the spare tire in return for the $50 dollar jump he put up his hand and said

I had done well as he could replace the tire and wheel for $10 dollar. It must have shown on his face so I related the remainder of the story. He just shook his head and called us dumb kids.

Once home I pulled out the tent and sleeping bags laying it out in the family room to dry off. Then I pulled out my cloths and emptied the pockets. At the bottom of my pocket, crumpled into a ball I found 5 dollars. I was disgusted and swore to be more careful in the future.

Kenny and I agreed that we had a grand adventure and would need to plan the next one soon. But this time we would be taking precautions with our funds and take the quirk out of the Pontiac's electrical system.

CHAPTER 22

Summer on the farm in Vermont

My mother and father both grew up in Northern Vermont on farms about 8 miles apart. Mom was the oldest of 8 children, 3 girls and 5 boys. Dad was the next to last of 2 girls and 6 boys.

We made our first visit to Vermont as a family during the summer of my sixth year. All of it was new to us with so many relatives we would hardly had a chance to remember names or relationships. Everyone knew us but my brother and I had not a clue who these people were.

We stayed at my maternal grandparents home located in Wolcott Vermont on what had at one time been an active farm. The barn and tool sheds were still located on the property but in disrepair. The back side of the property was used as a gravel quarry that eventually eroded what farm land there was.

My paternal grandparents lived on a farm up near Lake Elmore. My Grandfather passed away just before my birth so the farm was now run by my Aunt Barb and her husband Uncle Harold. Aunt Barb was a nice woman that looked over us boys when we came to work on the farm when I was eight. Aunt Barb and Uncle Harold have two children, one girl and one boy. When I came to work on the farm there daughter had married and moved away, there Son Bud was 18 years old and helped work the farm.

My paternal Grandmother lived in a single wide mobile home next door to the farm house. She was getting on in years but still set aside lots of time for us boys during our visits.

My brother and I spent most of our time helping Bud with the farm chores. The farm is about 250 acres and was given over primarily to raising dairy cows, though there was a field set aside for feed corn and a section containing a sugar orchard with the accompanying sugar shack. There were about 50 Holstein cows but at the time it seemed like an enormous dairy. If was far larger then my baby sitters farm that had only 4 cows. (A week later we went to visit our Uncle Jim and his son Jimmy's dairy farm had 500 dairy cows and an automated milking parlor.)

Each afternoon we made our way to the far end of a large pasture. Uncle Harold walked along with us always in his rubber boots, often stopping to pick wild straw berries growing in the pasture. Once we reached the farthest cow we started walking back towards the barn pushing the cows gentle ahead. The cows were anxious to be relieved of their milk and would walk towards the barn with full udders gently swaying.

Once at the barn each cow walked to their assigned spot to be temporarily held in a head stall. Each spot had a self-refilling water bowl that I found endlessly fun. When the paddle at the bottom was pushed more water would flood the bowl guaranteeing the cow an endless flow of water.

There was also a manger for each and we would carefully measure out a custom combination of grains to fit their dietary needs. The cows would dip there noses into the grain and with satisfied huffs and puffs consume this treat with contentment. The air filled with dust and the warmth generated by the cows would fill the barn causing overall serenity. The cows also filled the barn with the sharp odors from there generous deposits.

The milking was done by Uncle Harold and bud, both of whom were experienced at handling the cows. Each would use an individual milking machine, this was very different from Uncle Jim's large dairy with its automated milking parlor where the operator stood in a large concrete hole and reached up to attach each cow, the milk was automatically sent to the pasteurizer.

We helped Uncle Harold and Bud by cleaning the teats of each cow, and then Bud would come behind and hook up the cow to the milking machine, attached the hose to the vacuum connection and start the milker. Three milking machines for 50 dairy cows took over two hours to complete. After every couple of cows we would carry the milking machine to the pasteurizer to empty it into the huge stainless steel tank.

When the last cow was completed we released them back to the pasture. We weren't finished though, next came the clean-up. Each cows generates an amazing quantity of in just a couple hours. After spreading fresh hay we would make our way back to the house to help Aunt Barb in the kitchen. Just before meal time she handed me a milk pitcher. I would walk back to the milking parlor where the pasteurizer was located and the milk well chilled. Placing the pitcher under a faucet I watch fresh milk fill the vessel for our dinner.

One morning when I came to breakfast my Aunt Jessica had come to visit. I had met her before and unlike many other Vermonters she had made the 3000 mile drive to Hillsboro, Oregon on several occasions. I dearly loved her warmth, laughter and charm.

During a visit to Vermont many years later with my wife and 9 month old son I gained insight into the Vermonters perspective of distance. On the west coast we think nothing about hoping in the car and travelling 30 or even 40 miles to hit up a sale or make a visit. In Vermont you will find people that have only travelled that distance a handful of times in their life and never further than 50 miles from home.

In 1965 when one of my Uncles wanted to visit Oregon he called to ask about road conditions. All joking aside he asked how far they would have to travel by horse or if they could use a horse and wagon? With a grin on his face and suppressed laughter my father related how he could use the freeway system to reach our home. Even after he had drove the 3000 miles to our home he kept remarking upon the lack of horses and how good the roads were.

Aunt Jessica had come to take a horse ride with Aunt Barb and myself. Boy was I excited. Image I had to come all the way from the West coast, cowboy country to ride a horse in Vermont for the first time. We had a great time on the ride. During part of the ride we helped a neighbor heard there cows down the road to a new pasture. I felt like a real cowboy for the day.

The next day we started bringing in the hay. Bud had been out two weeks before with the tractor to bail the hay and leave it setting in the field ready to collect. Bud drove the tractor and my brother and I road on the hay wagon out to the field several times collecting and stacking the bales. Bud had to help with the top two rows since we were too short to toss the bales up.

My brother and I climbed to the top of the bales for the ride home enjoying the gentle swaying of the wagon and watching Bud at the tractor.

It was a long way up and I'm sure my mother would not have allowed it if she knew. At the barn we filled the barn loft by placing the bales on a conveyor that carried the to the barn loft where we each of us took turns to stacking bales.

Near the end of the day we were nearly done with the field we were working on so we stacked the hay on the wagon two rows higher then on previous trips. This finished the field so that we could go to a different field the next day.

On the way back to the barn we road on top of the bales as usual but Bud had to slow down where telephone wires crossed the rode. We lifted each wire up and over the hale bales, being careful to not knock a bale free. The ride back was different then the earlier ones as the hay was unstable and rocked back in forth as we made our way over the ruts in the road. When we came to a halt in front of the barn I had time to take sigh, thankful that we had made it safely back. The bales of hay decided to make one last gasp and opened under us dropping us all the way to the wagon bed, they then slammed shut over us locking us firmly in place. I calmly looked at the bales surrounding me and wondered what had happened. Before I could fully grasp my new location there was Bud furiously tossing bales every which way. As he reached me he was out of breath and gasped that he was sure he had killed me. We both rose up laughing and asked if we could do that again. Bud was not amused.

That evening we joined a group of local farmers and road the hay wagons out to a neighbor's field to collect his bales of hay. The trip back was happy with everyone chatting and laughing. That night I lay in bed and drifted off to sleep with a grin that wouldn't quit and sure that I wanted to spend my life farming.

CHAPTER 23

Tillamook Burn

The Tillamook Burn area in Oregon is located West of Portland in the Coast range located against the Pacific ocean. While growing up this was our playground. We gathered firewood in this area and collected cedar logs to convert to shakes for houses. This is where I learned to ride a dirt bike and where we on occasion held Boy Scout outings.

The Tillamook Burn lies approximately 50 miles West of Portland. The area gained its Burn designation due to the numerous fires that destroyed the area during the early part of the 20th century. The fires occurred in 1933, 1939, 1945 and 1951. The last one occurred about 15 years before the events that I write about here.

The 1933 fire started when a steel cable rubbed against a snag and burned 350,000 acres. The 1939 fire was blamed on logging operations but the cause was never firmly resolved and burned 190,000 acres. The 1945 fire burned 180,000 acres and was started by a careless smoker. Finally the 1951 fire burned 32,000 acres.

The area is mostly reforested and you have to look closely to discern that large fires had ever grown there. During the time of this story evidence of the fire was prevalent. There were hundreds of burned dead trees with their bark turning silver, we called these snags. Additionally there were large stumps of what must have been enormous trees. I still have a photograph of myself riding my tricycle around the top of one of these stumps while visiting my uncles logging operation.

During my time as a Boy Scout we spent many Saturdays planting 1000's of tree seedlings to recover this area. It's nice to see that we were successful, though the mix of tree species lacks the diversity that once was represented. There are far fewer cedar trees today than before the fires.

My father started a side roofing business harvesting the downed cedar snags in the Tillamook Burn. We hauled logs and rounds of aged cedar out using his old pickup truck outfitted with a home made winch and turn them into shakes using a mallet and a froe. The shakes were used to roof our home and to eventually roof the homes in the neighborhood.

We took our first trip to identify Cedar tree snags in the spring. As usual it was raining which means your going to get wet no matter what precautions are taken. We used the 1948 Chevrolet pickup to drive over the hills on the wet and muddy roads. Even though the truck was only two wheel drive we never got stuck, though there were a few times we had to get out and push to get moving.

Dad eventually upgraded to a newer but still old 1952 Chevrolet pickup. This truck also had two wheel drive but was blue instead of red. Dad built a winch and fabricated a new bumper on the front of the blue truck. The winch was used to haul snags out of the brush once they were cut down. The winch also meant we could pull ourselves out if we ever became stuck.

Saturday morning Dad woke my brother and I before the sun was up. I bundled myself up in old cloths and put on a jacket. After a quick bowl of cold cereal we were in the pickup and headed for the Tillamook Burn. An hour later we would be turning off onto dirt side roads. Today's target was a previously located dead cedar tree. The Home lite chainsaw made quick work of the snag, dropping it to the ground where it could be cut into rounds. My brother and I would roll the rounds out of the woods and down to the pickup where we loaded them in the pickup bed stacking and packing in as many as we could. The winch was only used if we couldn't work where the snag was dropped. Eventually Dad fabricated a trailer to accommodate larger loads and fewer trips.

Once home we hustled to unload the truck and get ready to go back out. We usually made this trip twice a day depending on if Dad and Mom had something planned for the evening.

The following year our neighbor joined us with his son. It was nice having the extra help but it also meant we now had two trucks and two trailers to fill on each trip.

Late that summer we found an enormous snag. It would have been a revival for a redwood tree though it was missing quite a bit off the top. It took all day working around the tree with chainsaw to eventually have it fall away from the road. We had enough time to load up and make it home in the dark. Our loads barely scratched the resources of the snag.

That night Mom and Dad had a card party. They had 12 friends that would alternate homes for the parties. They setup three tables and played pinochle until late in the evening. I would later learn to play pinochle and fill in for one of the people when needed. They were loud affairs with lots of laughter and joking. My Mother could be heard throughout the house when she really got excited.

The next Saturday we returned to the big tree but much to our dismay it was gone. It must have been a regular logging outfit that came in and removed the giant. I hadn't really sure how we were going to get it all out as part of it stretched over a gully. I had visions of standing on the snag as it plummeted into the valley.

Over the period of several years we gathered enough cedar to shingle 6 houses. We would use mallets and throe's to slice off shingles from each round. Cedar is a nice grained wood that loves to be split. We worked at this for several months and used up several Throes. Dad put his skills to work and started making our own Throe's. They were quite a bit heavier but compensated by slicing through the wood much easier.

We found many interesting areas in the mountains. One of my favorites was the look-out mountain fire tower. The tower stood 5 stories with a set of stairs zigzagging to the top. Once on top there was walk way that went all around the tower. From the top of the tower on a clear day we could see the Pacific Ocean.

Another favorite spot was the grader. The grader had been used to smooth the roads but due to an accident it had ran off the road and down a steep embankment. The slope was very steep and the grader too heavy to recover. The grader started out yellow but over the years started to blend into the forest. The last time I saw it I was 19 and took a friend up, it was very difficult to find.

CHAPTER 24

The Mummy of Forest Street

Our summers started with Strawberry picking on the local farms. The farmers sent out busses to the neighborhoods to pick up groups of kids waiting in cool morning dawn and returned them to hot midday pickup locations. Each kid took their lunch usually in a paper sack that included a frozen can of soda pop. By the time lunch rolled around the block of ice soda would melt, hopefully.

At lunch I went back to the bus for my lunch but the big kids wouldn't let me on. I was only 9 at the time and had no patience for the taunting. I went back and forth between the front door and back watching them dangle my lunch sack temptingly, but they held the doors against me. With a final resolve I kicked out the window of the bus door. You can bet that got those kids attention and got me my lunch.

Later the farmer Mr. Vanderzanden came to me as I was picking berries. He spoke calmly and elicited the complete story of the broken window from me. I was never punished but the older boys had their pay docked for the damages. My father was not as calm and generous.

Many years later during college summer break I found myself back at the same farm. I was the typical college student with no money but time on my hands. To my amazement Mr. Vanderzanden down my row, crouched down and started to help me pick berries. Then a quiet voice he said David, how are you? It had been 9 years since I saw him last but he still remembered me and more importantly the bus window.

All that season I worked hard picking more and more flats each day, I needed all the money I could get. My row partner Jill kept urging me on to pick more than Greta who was top picker. Jill was a few years younger and the sister of a classmate. We spent hours conversing and getting to know each other. Over the following years my memory would return to our quiet times together. I regretted not having her contact information as she became a good friend.

The first day I picked 17 pallets, an exciting record beating my previous best of 12. Greta the top picker in the field picked more. I started to arrive a bit earlier each day as Great also came early. Each day was a repeat of the last, I would out pick my previous days record only to have Greta pick more. It was really great fun and Mr. Vanderzanden was there egging me on each day providing frequent updates on Greta's progress.

On the last day of picking the big day came. I smashed the field record as well as my own by picking 50 flats. My hands had flown snagging each berry, popping off the top and gently dropping them in to the flat. I made sure each flat was clean of dirt and all the berries looked good.

Finally I had beat Greta, it was a good feeling to know I had made so much money. The thrill however was short lived, ending soon after the arrival of Mr. Vanderzanden. He had a big grin on his face and after a long pause asked me if I knew Greta and her 4 kids all put there pallets onto one card. Jill laughed hysterically holding her stomach with tears streaming from her eyes. I was sure we were going to have to find her a clean pair of jeans. Mr. Vanderzanden just cracked that big smile in the middle of his sun burned head. No doubt about it, I had been had.

When I was 10 for some reason the older boys in the neighborhood decided to pick at Hertel's farm. I picked there for 3 years and had decided to give it up. They picked their fields past maturity and the berries were small making it difficult to earn much money. I liked the short bus trip but not the strict rules.

My brother had moved on to Spangler's and raved about the giant berries and best of all four free Craigmont sodas every day. It was a 1 hour bus ride but after seeing that my little brother was making more money I jumped to Spangler's where rule were less strict. Mr. Spangler was kindly and spent time getting to know each picker. The bushes were huge and required a picker on each side. The rows were so long they started a pair of kids on each end. They also let you eat as many berries as you wanted knowing that by the second day you would have gorged yourself and lost interest.

After berry picking season we spent much of our summer vacations on our bikes. There wasn't much for 10 speed bikes and everyone was riding one speeds. We impersonated motorcycles by attaching playing cards with clothes pins so that they rattled across our spokes. We also played baseball down on the Baloney's property but after the first week came up short of pitchers.

The field was homemade and smaller than regulation which meant the pitcher's mound was closer to the plate then a full size field. With no helmets or cups or any safety gear the pitcher was exposed to line drives.

It became a real challenge to pitch and dodge the ball before receiving a solid blow to the groin. My brother hung in there longer than most using his unique pitching method. He would wind up and throw the ball overhand followed by throwing himself to into dirt face first.

After a dry dusty game on the field I decided to take a shower to clean the crud off. While I was enjoying the warm water and preparing the soap and wash cloth I was doused with cold water laced with ice cubes. I gasped as the air left my body, then slowly took a ragged breath back. I heard the bathroom door close and quickly retreating footsteps. I burst from the shower not bothering with a towel and raced after my brother. When I hit the living room there stood Mack Buldony, his feet rooted to the floor and his mouth hanging open, too scared to move a muscle. I could see the front screen door swinging shut and my brother at full gallop racing away. I applied the brakes before racing into the front yard, turned, glared at Mack and went back to my shower deep in thought. This could not go unpunished.

Our next door neighbor's children were all much older except for Bird who was only 3 years older than I. Bird was a nick name applied by his brother due to his skinny legs. Several years later I went to work for Bird at Hillsboro Cabinets as a kitchen cabinet installer. Bird would crank up the song Free Bird in the shop at least twice a day making sure we knew his nick name.

Bird's father Nels was a nice man though with five children he would sometimes loose his patience. Nels would visit the Oregon coast and while there pick up a large bag of oysters. When he got home he would sit in the back yard, shell then eat the oysters. Neighborhood boys would frequently sit with him, he would challenge each of us to eat a fresh oyster. Overall he was a nice neighbor and patient with us boys and Dad's home projects.

One summer day as I exited my front door, I saw Bird sitting in his front yard. He was leaning back casually with legs crossed and propping himself up with his arms. I stopped to chat with him and in the process learned they had a guest staying in the shed out back. The shed was at the back fence of their property where the driveway ended and could be seen from the street. This fellow staying there had been injured in an accident and didn't want anyone bothering him. Bird explained that they had wrapped his head in badges until he healed up.

After a while a large group of boys had gathered in Bird's front yard. Not unusual as we all played together during the summer months. There was a distinct shortage of girls in the neighborhood and the ones that were there frequently joined us.

Everyone was interested in this fellow staying in the back shed, three of us brave souls decided to go have a look and check on him. We walked quietly down the driveway crouching lower and lower, moving slower with each step. Bird had built up the suspense to such pitch that our fear unconsciously slowed us to a crawl. Soon we were bunched together and hardly moving ten feet from the shed door. It was at this point the shed door banged open and there stood a man wrapped in badges with green gore dripping from the edges. Our response was instantaneous and simultaneous. Like at pack of frightened coyotes we ran down the driveway and into the street causing the boys waiting to scatter.

Some of the other boys with more curiosity then brains wanted a look for themselves. When they had worked up there courage they headed down the driveway bunching up much like the first group. It didn't take long and they came scrambling back down the driveway.

Bird did a good job of keeping up the excitement and uncertainty, but eventually after a few hours we found out the truth. Birds older brother dressed up in rags to create some excitement and alleviate boredom. It was all in good fun.

Bird's father Nels approached my Dad one day and asked if we could take down the cherry tree in their back yard. This tree was beside the mummy's shed. One cool autumn day we ventured into Bird's yard with ladders, chainsaw, ropes and pulleys. Dad worked his way up the ladder cutting off and dropping large branches to us boys who quickly stacked the limbs to the side. Eventually Dad was down to the trunk and an one especially large branch. The trunk of the cherry tree was large enough that my brother and I could just reach around it to join hands.

Dad setup a pulley at the top of the trunk about 15 feet above the branch, then he used a rope to tie off the large branch, loop it through the pulley and bring it back down to the ground where my brother and I would be able to keep the branch from dropping and hurting anyone. The pulley system was setup to reduce the pulling power required to lower the branch to the ground. We were about 14-15 at the time and were confident we could lower the branch to the ground unaided.

Dad fired up the chain saw making his first cut on the bottom side of the branch. He then repositioned himself on the ladder and started his cut to the top of the branch near the trunk. My brother and I got a good hold on the rope so that we could control the branch. The chain saw reached the bottom cut, the branch swung free and dropped swiftly to the ground as if the two of us were of no consequence. My brother and I shot up in the air where we hung from the rope 15 feet in the air. Well ok, maybe we should have gotten some more help.

The fact is we had gotten use to handling old cedar snags. Cedar is much lighter being less dense then cherry. Hanging from the rope I didn't see much humor in the situation, Dad on the other hand was giving us the horse laugh.

That night the time for revenge had come. I heard my brother coming up the stairs and then getting ready for bed. We each slept nearly naked except for our underwear. I didn't have long to wait before a blood curdling scream smote the air. My revenge for the cold shower was complete. Earlier that day I had gathered a arm load of metal hangers and introduced them to the cold of the freezer. I waited until my brother started brushing his teeth in preparation for bed time.

I gathered up my now frigid hangers and spread them between the sheets of his bed. There they laid well insulated waiting for my brother to slip between the sheets.

CHAPTER 25

Summer Olympics

Looking back you could say the Forest Street Olympics started when my brother decided to exercise Mr. Holt's gate. A group of boys took turns hanging from the fence and back and forth until it finally broke from its hinges. When Mrs. Holt came to talk to my father about what had happen my brother stood there and said that wasn't him but was me. Mrs. Holt laughed at him and pointed her finger saying, young man I saw what you did, it was not your brother. Dad repaired the fence better then new and it started a long wonderful friendship with the Holts.

Many years later I was visiting with Mrs. Holt when she was in her 90's. Sharp as a tack, she brought up the gate incident. "You're brother thought he could blame it on you, but I know who did it."

Though he passed many years ago I can still hear the echo of Mr. Holt's deep laugh and remember the pranks he played on my Mom over the years. He was also a member of the examiners for my Eagle Scout award and he was as proud of me as if he had been my own father.

That summer my Dad brought home an old girls bike. This was the type with the low slooping brace between the handle bars and seat as well as large balloon tires. While unloading the bikeI came out to see what he had. To my dismay I learned this was to be my bike, oh the humanity, oh the embarrassment. I was to riding a girls bike while all my friends had cool bikes. The bike was far too large for me having been built for adults and way too big for me. Everyone else in the neighborhood was riding Stingray bikes and it's what I really wanted. I wanted the banana seat and three speed shift.

With no choice I rode the girl's bike. While sitting on the seat I couldn't reach the peddles. if peddling I couldn't sit on the seat. While riding with my mother and brother we were coming down Grant Street next to what would become Hare Field but was a large open area. The road was under construction and was covered with a compressed layer of gravel. I lost control of the bike, slipped off the seat and hit the gravel with my bare knees braking the bike to a halt. I was wearing shorts and took a full load of gravel to the knees, blood was pouring down my legs and filling my shoes. The pain was excruciating but nothing in comparison to what awaited me at home. Mom helped me back on my bike and I painfully peddle home.

When we arrived home Dad grabbed his arsenal of medical tools. Tweezers, gauze, hydrogen peroxide, antiseptic powder and bag balm and set to work on my knees. He pulled a dozen pieces of grave out of each knee and after each would was removed would douse the wound with hydrogen peroxide. Each douse was more painful than the fall from the bike. I would moan and Dad would tell me to suck it up, "Can't be that bad". I could feel the phantom pain in my knees for years afterwards. Also turns out that Dad had purchased the wrong hydrogen peroxide. He used the hairdresser strength which is 4-5 times higher in concentration and in pain generation.

There was a positive side to the girl's bike event and that was I got a boys bike that fit me. The bike had one speed but was much easier to ride.

Several years later I purchased my first bike with money earned working at my Uncle's hardware store in Sheridan Oregon. It was a 10-speed Huffy that I rode through my sophomore year in college. The frame snapped at multiple locations.

My Uncle Hugh's hardware store in Sheridan Oregon was called Ivy's when they purchased it and renamed it to the family name. My Uncle, Aunt and there youngest boy moved out from Vermont, settling in Sheridan. I had a great time working with my Uncle and Aunt and spending time with my older cousin. We tarred the roof, made repairs on the building and clerked in the store. At lunch Uncle Hugh would send me to the local burger joint to get my lunch and to pick up a burger for him. For my Uncle there was also his favorite Orange Crush soft drink.

When I returned from lunch and started clerking one day I led a customer back to the nail bins to help him find what he needed. On the way back I saw my cousin lying in the isle, I assumed he was sleeping. The customer missed a beat; he lifted his foot to step over him and with hardly a glance continued back to the nails. Later my cousin related what had brought him to such a lowly state.

My cousin decided to mouth off to his father, my Uncle, and refused to do the work he was asked to perform. My uncle was a short man and my cousin was six foot and still growing. Uncle balled up his fist and tapped my cousin on the chin, dropping him to the floor and knocking him out to boot. My cousin related that he was wrong to act the way he did and from that day forward treated his father with greater respect.

My Uncle had me pick a bicycle out of the store catalog, I selected a fancy 10-speed Huffy. He then ordered it and when it arrived assembled the bike. They my Aunt and Uncle drove up to Hillsboro to deliver my new bike. The bike was special in that I had earned it and my Uncle showed his appreciation for my help. I rode the bike for many years, It was a great bike and carried me for 1000's of miles.

One summer Daryl Bulldony setup a broad jump on their property. We had fun taking turns to see who could jump highest without knocking off the bar. It was very official looking but lacked one important component, the heavy pad in landing zone. Instead of the pad we made due with hard packed dirt. I know we were bruised and scraped but everyone showed up each day to take part again.

A few days later Daryl added another event. He brought a pole so that we could pole vault over the same stick. Not thinking about it we took turns going higher and higher landing in the same hard packed dirt. Eventually it was just plain scary to look down from several feet and say to yourself, "this is going to hurt!" Yet amazingly there were no broken bones, but lots of bruises and scrapes.

We also practiced sprints and set out a cross country course that we all ran each day. Eventually the day for the completion arrived. Daryl brought out his stop watch and we all ran for all we were worth to prove who was the fastest. Then it was high jump, pole vault, shot put and finally the cross country race. I don't remember who won. I only had a two block walk but I dragged myself home well and truly exhausted but looking forward to doing it again.

CHAPTER 26

Dodger and the Whippet

The neighbor's puppy, a whippet 6 months old, wandered into the yard mid-summer.

My introduction to the intruder was a thump on the back of the knee by a cold wet nose. Being busy I told him to get going, get out of here! I have a fondness for dogs but after losing our Newfoundland I just haven't had the heart to become attached again. The Newfy is big, but also loyal, protective and very loveably. There is always enough dog to go around for a family petting session.

The puppy wandered around the corner of the house and within 3 feet of Dodger sitting on the back step. Dodger really likes dogs; while alive our big Newfoundland Rex was his best friend. He's always friendly with dogs as long as they reciprocate. Unfortunately our other neighbors Springer Spaniel found out the hard way. It's now been 5 years since the

Spaniel stopped coming as far as our shared fence. Today the Spaniel settles for keeping his distance and allows Dodger to use as much of their yard as he pleases.

About 15 minutes later I was on the other side of the house spreading corn gluten meal to keep the weeds at bay. Dodger wandered out ahead of me in a pleasant mood, enjoying the spring sunshine. Then poof, there was the little whippet. He slid quietly up to Dodger nose quivering, wet nose stretched forth. Well he did it, he dared to go where no other dog before him had gone. He performed the doggie to doggie greeting upon Dodger.

Dodger is mostly an outdoor cat by choice. His nerves are finely tuned to close tolerances; his limbs are powerful, ending in razor blade claws. It's this finally tuned instrument that has allowed him to survive outside with coyotes, cougars, bears, hawks and eagles.

Dodger being a wild creature without hesitation reacted instantly to the whippet's wet nose. With powerful thrusts of his limbs he darted up the nearest cedar tree without once looking back. Only knowing that his survival relied on responding quickly. He went up the tree as if he was running across open ground, his claws scrabbling and grasping the bark of the cedar tree. 15 feet above the ground, he paused to look back at his attacker.

The whippet stood with tail slowing swinger back in forth, a witness to the incredible speed of the cat. Dodger with disgust dropped from the tree, a dog, nothing but a common dog. Dodger calmly walked to the whippet and let him know in no uncertain terms that he had crossed the lines of civility. The whippet quickly retired with Dodger hot upon his tail.

The young whippet has not been seen for several weeks but were certain he will return. Young dogs are forever curious and quickly forget the lessons administered.

CHAPTER 27

Pioneering

One of the benefits of being a Boy Scout in the 70's with a Scout Master having extensive outdoor experience are the varied activities you experience. We spent time learning and performing activities that made us better community members, able to survive in the urban kitchen, understand financing and budgeting.

Rarely taught now are Morse code and semaphore signaling. Morse code is a method of signaling that uses only dots and dashes. Semaphore is performed using two flags, one in each hand. Letters and number are sent by varying the angle at witch you held your arms. Both of these techniques can be import to survival in the wilderness.

We also learned knot tying, camping, back packing, hiking, outdoor cooking, first aid, swimming, sailing, boating, canoeing, fitness, conservation, orienteering as well as dozens of others. The goal is to create and individual who becomes a well-rounded adult. My first experiences cooking was learning over an open fire that is challenging in of itself.

Our Scout Master Mr. West was well versed in Astronomy, the study of the stars and there locations. Mr. West was father of 3 girls and had become involved with Boy Scouts as a method of adding sons to his life. After serving in the U.S. Army during World War II he obtained employment with Portland General Electric as a line and service man for many years. He was an experienced carver and spent many hours in his home workshop creating signs and carving various wilderness scenes.

On our back packing excursions we frequently found ourselves beyond the reach of city lights and at high elevations in the Cascade Mountains of Oregon. After setting up our tents then preparing our meals over an open cook fire we would sit around the fire talking until the stars started to appear. Mr. West would lead us away from the fire to a clearing where we could gaze up at the stars. Using his flash light he would point out the constellations until the sky became so covered with stars that it was difficult to discern one from the next.

(A note here to other back packers: Yes we used camp fires and were safely taught to do so. Today we use compact stoves that are safer and more environmentally friendly. Unfortunately at the time I was a Boy Scout there were no compact stoves. The option was to carry a 20+ pound metal two burner gas stove along with the fuel. Not a viable option.)

Each year we went on several camping and back packing trips as well as a summer camp. Summer camp was a week away from our homes at Boy Scout designated camps. While at camp we were able to complete requirements for rank. Rank started at Tenderfoot and you then worked your way up to First class. These ranks didn't require merit badges but had their own list of requirements. After First class you would earn merit badges for ranks of Star, Life and finally Eagle. Summer camp was a great place to earn some of the more difficult merit badges like canoeing and archery.

The first summer camp I attended was Camp Baldwin located East of Mount Hood in the Mount Hood National Forest. This a dry pine forest compared to the wetter fir forests we have in the Willamette Valley. In 1969 when our troop arrived at the camp we were assigned a site called Wolf Run. We shared tents that were erected on elevated wood platforms.

In some camps everyone ate together at a dining hall but at Camp Baldwin the food and recipes were delivered to your camp. Each boy then would have the opportunity to prepare and cook the meal over an open fire. My meal to prepare came up on Tuesday night and included hamburgers. While preparing the burgers under the scrutiny and criticisms of the other boys I made a monstrous mistake. Stooping over the grill issued a cup with a lid to lightly salt each one of the burgers with salt. As I did this the cover came free along with a large quantity of salt that created an impressive mound on the burger. With a gasp, all the boys drew back as if an explosion was imminent. This was followed with a unanimous decision declaring the burger was now mine. I scraped off what salt I could and found and while slightly salty is was still a good burger.

While there I spent time learning how to row a canoe and row boats. There small lake was perfect as the water stayed very calm. Later in the week Mr. West had arranged for all of us to go for horse rides. This was fun, we rode the trails through the pine forests surround the camp. This is a special activity as only two Scout camps in the world provide riding horses and opportunity to earn the horsemanship merit badge.

Many years later my son and I became involved in the Boy Scout Explorer post that took care of the horses at the Butte Creek ranch near Scott Mills Oregon in the Willamette Valley. Each year instead of trucking the horses out to Camp Baldwin and then back they have a Horse Trek. Everyone, even those not a part of Scouting can pay to participate in the ride to Camp Baldwin in the spring or the return trip in the fall to Butte Creek. Each person is assigned a horse to care for and then set out on a 150 mile journey to camp Baldwin. This is a great experience and many of the wranglers are Scouts that assist in horse education and rides throughout the year. Without these Scouts they would be unable to provide the horse related activities.

While at camp Mr. West brought blocks of wood, knives and carving tools that he used to teach us how to carve. Fortunately he also brought a lot of Band-Aids but still it was a wonderful experience that I occasionally still perform. That year Mr. West had seen the sign for our camp site "Wolf Run" lying on the ground broken, so he undertook to create a new one. He found a long log and after cleaning off the branches creates a long flat section near one end. On this end he carved the letters "Wolf Run" vertically down the pole. We joined together digging to setup the new sign near the entrance. Amazingly 45 years later I walked by the camp site and there was the sign still standing.

Each evening there was camp fire where we watched or performed skits and sang songs. Afterwards we would return to our camp in the dark. Along the way large toads hopped out of our path traveling as fars as 6 feet at a jump. When it came time for the creature race we captured a toad know he could win the race with one. All of the creatures were placed in the center of a circle drawn in the dirt. Our win was not to be, the toad fell asleep while all the other critters crawled for the edge of the circle. After the race Mr. West stated we might have won if the race were held after dark since this toad was obviously a night creature.

Each year there was a camporee where all the scouts from local troops gathered at a remote camp site and would participate in events to demonstrate skills. One of my favorites was building a fire, they would tie a string across two sticks with the string about three fee off the ground. Teams would then each take a turn carefully building a fire up until it was hot enough to burn through the string. This usually took 10-15 minutes. Mr. West walked us through the goal of the exercise, burn through the string. The trick was not to setup a nice campfire or cooking fire but to build a fast burning fire. He showed us how to build up the fire material using very light fine material stacked to within an inch of the string. The fire would burn fast and not provide a lasting fire. Acting as a judge at a nearby event that year, I watched as boys worked hard building up fires that would burn through the string. The best time I had observed to this point was 15 minutes. I saw my brothers patrol lined up as the next participants but at that moment was distracted by the event I was judging. When I next I turned around I saw the boys light there fire witch swept up in 5 foot flames and immediately parted the string.

At one of these events we were taught how to start fires using two sticks, we all became quite proficient until it took us less than two minutes to start a fire. There were lots of people that seemed amazed to see it work. Once you know how it's not very hard. Later that year we performed demonstrations at the fairgrounds drawing crowds to watch. It was at this event that I became very sick and for the next couple of weeks found myself constantly coughing.

After school the next week it all caught up to me and when arrived home I turned up the heat and huddled over the floor register under a pile of blankets. When my father arrived home from work it was not hard to determine something was wrong. He said the house was over 90 degrees inside. He found me under the pile of blankets sick from pneumonia. He bundled me up and took me to the doctor's office. Afterwards I spent a full week recovering at home and was very glad not to be coughing any more.

By far my favorite scout event was pioneering themed weekend. It started out with Mr. West, my father and some of the boys taking a trip out to the woods where we cleared away brush and cut fallen trees into logs 6-8 feet. We worked all weekend each of us wondering why this was needed. Turned out we were preparing the space for the next camporee.

Two weeks later we returned to the area we cleared. Mr. West had piled the back of his truck with ropes of various lengths and sizes. The ropes were to practice our construction skills in what is known as pioneering. The ropes and timbers are used to build various constructs that made camp life easier or to overcome obstacles such as rope bridges.

We setup our tents and fire rings at the location designated for our troop. This year the events would be judged for each troop rather than the smaller sub groups called patrols. The first thing we constructed was a suspended rope bridge. Without a river or canyon we used the shallow dip in the middle of our camp. Two logs on each end were lashed into a cross, and then a heavy rope was anchored across the logs to make the foot path of the bridge. This was followed by two ropes acting as hand rails and shorter ropes tied between handrail and foot path for stability.

We then broke into smaller groups to build smaller items, signal tower, wash stand and kitchen table. Two of the older boys created a three sided shelter by notching and fitting sticks together with no ropes. When completed we had an impressive display. The judges came around early Saturday afternoon and judged each of the troops on the quality of knots and lashings. After judging we were free to roam around to other troops to see what they had done.

The rope bridge was very popular with the boys and adults and most everyone in camp crossed it more than once. At one time one of our boys thought it would be better if it crossed over water, using a dish pan filled with water; he placed it under the bridge. It looked quite ludicrous a tiny pan of water under a long rope bridge. Eventually someone showing off slipped from the bridge and smacked into the water, I guess it was bound to happen.

I made many friends in Scouting and over the years we occasionally found time to catch up. But with the nature of human interactions we eventually drifted apart with our own needs and ambitions. I occasionally run into one of them. Last fall I was pulled over by a police officer. I think you all know the feeling as your heart races. Fortunately it was an old friend from scouting that pulled me over to say howdy and give me a heart attack.

CHAPTER 28

Drive to Canada

Shortly after graduating from high school, I and three friends decided to take a June adventure. My best friend Kenny provided the old blue Pontiac and our good friend Mac went along as a sort of celebration. Mac is extremely intelligent, he could play instruments by ear with no lessons and he was brilliant with electronics and he ended up having a knack for making money.

Mac made his money refurbishing homes, shortly after high school he a decrepit home for very little as it was in retched shape and had no foundation. The money for the down payment came interestingly enough while he was riding along with us on a washer-dryer delivery. Kenny's father owned a local appliance store and for a few years we performed appliance repair and delivery. The pay wasn't great but we got free meals and a pickup to drive.

On the trip with mac along we were to drop off a new freezer and pick up an old freezer. The old freezer was from a prior era and was much heavier then what we normally handled so Mac went along. We off loaded the new freezer with no problem but the old one was solid, if felt like the frozen contents had not been removed. We opened her up and found it empty so off we went grunting and huffing to just lift one end into the back of the pickup. Once on the truck the back of the half ton dipped alarmingly. While Kenny and I tied down the load Mac went back to talk to the home owner. She had an old jukebox in the garage that she had used as a bird cage and then dumped it in the garage when the birds passed away. Mac purchased it from her for $20. It was covered in dirt and grease not to mention the mess that the birds had left behind.

Later that day we returned for the jukebox and hauled it to Mac's parents where he took it a part and cleaned every inch until it appeared new. With records added and a new needle for the turn table, it ran like new and was near new condition on the outside. It was then that I recognized the jukebox for the old television sitcom Happy Days, not the same one but surely a spitting image of the same. This was the jukebox that Arnold had at his drive-in and was highly sought after by collectors. Mac sold it for $7000 witch was enough to purchase his first run down home. That was what I call one good barn find.

Mac rebuilt the home adding a foundation; he sold the home and used the money to purchase more run down homes. Unlike today, in 1977 there was little competition for these old homes so people were happy to unload them. After a few years Mac eventually purchased and renovated his final home, closed all the projects down and came out several million dollars ahead and in a position to do what he wanted.

That summer Kenny, Mac and I planned on taking Kenny's 1969 Pontiac Lemans on a trip to Vancouver Island in Canada. This island is off the western shore of British Columbia Canada end encompasses more than 12,000 square miles. We needed to leave early in the morning to make the 5 hour drive to reach the early morning ferry that left Port Angeles Washington and went to Victoria Canada on Vancouver Island.

We didn't get off as early as we planned and it was my fault. I had set my alarm for 2:30 AM and slept right through. What eventually woke me was someone tossing pebbles against my window and finally noting the alarm beeping. I hung my head out the second story window and Mac told me if I still wanted to go I better get moving. I dressed quickly and grabbed my bag but we still had a start later then we planned. Its 264 miles to Port Angeles in Washington and only about two thirds is on interstate freeways.

We headed towards Portland Oregon on highway 26 and merged on to I5 north headed towards Seattle. Kenny pushed the Pontiac up to 90 mph as we passed through Vancouver Washington, not to be confused with Vancouver British Columbia where the 2010 winter Olympics was held. The road was clear and when we had no problems so he pushed it up to 120 mph. We stopped at a gas station in Olympia and switch drivers, I put my foot to the floor and when we reached Tacoma took highway 16 across the Tacoma narrows bridge. I have never driven on public roadways at such speeds since and looking back it scares me senseless today.

The original Tacoma narrows bridge was known as Galloping Gertie because of how the bridge would sway and drop up and down in the wind. Engineers declared it safe but eventually it collapsed in to Puget Sound on November 7, 1940. If interested you can find it on youtube.com "Tacoma Narrows Bridge Collapse "Galloping' Gertie".

We made the trip in time in time for the early morning ferry, we were the third car on what would be a sold out passage. To this day I'm still amazed we weren't picked up and most likely should have been. I had noted during the drive that Mac who had spent the trip in the back seat laid down and strapped on all three seat belt tightly. Idiots like us now know that at 120 mph telephone poles really did look like a picket fence. I can safely say that trip fulfilled my need for speed, but not for Kenny. Kenny would later purchase an extremely fast British sports car and push it up over 160 mph on the track at Portland International Raceway but eventually even he reached the full Mark. Mac drove for a few months then near his 19th birthday gave up driving and to this day has never taken it up again.

The sun had just come up as we pulled in as the third car in line for the ferry. Soon we were on our way across the Strait of Juan de Fuca. I was sea sick for the first time in my life even though the waters were calm. I had been out on the ocean in small boats many times and had no problems but the gentle rocking of the ferry was too much for me. Before I got worse I purchase some saltine crackers to nibble upon and made the remainder of the journey with no further issues.

When we reach the city of Victoria it took a while to disembark since the ferry was filled to capacity there was a long wait as each vehicle cleared customs. We were then free to explore Victoria. Victoria is a beautiful city that is also the capitol of the British Columbia province. This is also the home of the famous Butchart Gardens that opened in 1904.

For the next leg of the journey along the inland highway we stayed to the speed limit and made several stops to enjoy the beautiful views of the inland waterway. The weather was damp but the sun poked out enough to make the journey pleasant. We made a stop for gas where the station had one of the old bubble gas pumps still in operations.

We reached our destination, Campbell River where the road ended as it was closed for bridge repairs. Kenny had worked for a company once summer at a logging camp on one of the nearby islands. Our plan was to call them and they would pick us up. The call was made but no one picked up the phone. Darkness was approaching so we started hunting for a campground or public area where we could sleep for the night. Fortunately we found a family that was willing to let us use their back yard to pitch our two man tent. That night we somehow managed to squeeze the three of us into the tent and find sleep.

In the morning we awoke soaking wet from the overnight rain. The rear tent pole had been knocked down and the tent lay on top of our sleeping bags where the rain had pooled up and leaked into the sleeping bags. We spent the morning blaming each other for having big feet that knocked down the pole. The sun was out and the weather cool but we soon dried out and warmed up. Kenny made another call to the logging camp but again no answer.

After a quick breakfast we headed back to Victoria taking our time. We stopped at a small town and tried out the local gambling. They had hundreds of machines to play Pachinko, not very entertaining was our assessment.

We arrived in Victoria and had to wait a few hours for a ferry. We used this time to view some of the historical buildings such as the Empress Hotel that opened in 1908. The ferry ride was uneventful and we soon drove onto the dock at Port Angeles Washington and headed south. Near Tacoma we merged into I5 southbound.

We held to the speed limit and a good thing we did. Washington sets up speed traps. If you're not familiar with this operation I have included a short description. The police hide a radar operator in an unmarked car or behind some bushes. When you pass they note your speed and license number. Some distance down the freeway and out of site are several police cars lined up. Each officer pulls over a car identified by the radar operator. It appears to be quite affective but good fortune smiled on us when we started to turn into smart drivers on the trip home.

CHAPTER 29

Fishing with Uncle Al

Almerion, also known as Uncle Al was my father's oldest sibling. Born in 1918, Uncle Al was 12 years older than my father. He worked at several different jobs his primary being a farm mechanic. As a farm mechanic he was called upon by the Vermont farmers whenever there was a repair required on equipment that they couldn't perform themselves.

He was also known for his ponds through-out central Vermont many of which still remain. The pond next to his home was stocked with large and healthy trout. This pond was fed by a small creek that constantly fed the pond and kept the water moving preventing mosquito larva from forming. Some time around the year 2000 Vermont had heavy snow and flooding ensued exasperated by heavy rains. The pond overflowed washed all those record fish in to the ponds and nearby rivers where the fisherman enjoyed catching record size trout.

Uncle Al had several hidden fishing spots and a fishing lodge where he escaped to enjoy a few quiet hours. My father took us to one of these spots during a trip to Vermont.

We drove some distance through the country side until we reached an unremarkable stretch of road. There were no signs or indicators where we pulled over on the side of the road. Witch tackle boxes and fishing poles we marched off into the trees. The undergrowth was sparse but lacked any indication of a trial.

One mile from the road we came to a natural lake. We found one of Uncle Al's boats tied to a log looking worse for wear. We jumped aboard, bailed out the excess water and pushed off from shore. The lake consumed about 10 acres, was surrounded by beautiful maple trees. The water was clear and allowed up to see the fish that made the lake home.

My brother and I started fishing and immediately had fish on the line. We caught dozens of sun fish until we eventually grew tired of reeling them into the boat. Unfortunately we later learned that these were an invasive species and were quite inedible.

These were the first fish I ever caught; I had proven to be a poor fisherman even when we took a charter boat out of Depot Bay Oregon. Everyone on the boat including my brother caught there limit of salmon. My count was zero, nada.

During this time Dad trolled for bass along the shore. While we rowed quietly into each inlet he would cast into the water in shadowy locations where the bass liked to hangout. He seemed to have quite a bit of fun but was unable to hook a single one.

Eventually we returned to the car quite satisfied with our quiet, peaceful day.

Later in the week Uncle Al announced that he had time available to go fishing and would like to take us up to his fishing lodge.

We left early Friday morning and after a long drive parked at the end of a dirt road where a trail led into the trees. After winding through the trees for one quarter of a mile we came to Uncle Al's hunting lodge. This was a small 15 foot square single story building and nothing like what I had anticipated.

Uncle Al walked us around the "cabin" and showed us how he had installed sheets of metal over the corners and edges to keep the hedge hogs from chewing up the structure (Hedge hogs being the local equivalent for porcupine). Porcupines are numerous in Vermont and can prove to be a nuance as they will gnaw and chew on just about anything.

In order to reduce the population of porcupines a type of marten called a fisher was introduced from Canada. The fisher is larger than a marten being 8-12 pounds. There primary diet is rabbits and porcupines.

After looking over the cabin we continued down the trail to the fishing grounds. This was an area with meandering streams and small ponds. The surrounding area was moras of a marsh, squishy earth and water.

Along the way Uncle Al saw a porcupine up a tree. He handed the gun to my younger brother who aimed and pulled the trigger. The porcupine dropped into the brush. Uncle Al turned to me and said "you get the next one".

We fished but as usual I failed to catch any fish.. The mosquitoes were vicious and swarmed us in the thousands. A bare arm would be covered with 100's of the little nuances in seconds. The great state of Montana jokingly claims the mosquito as there state bird but that day I would of said that Vermont was giving them a run for their money.

My brother and I were quite miserable and soon lost all interest in fishing. Dad produced an ancient small bottle of insect repellent from his pocket witch we liberally applied. This helped slightly but by that time we were covered with welts. We tried to start a fire so that we could stand in the smoke but the material was to wet.

At one point Dad showed up with a large leaf on his head to keep the voracious insects from decorating his bald pate. The leaf was covered with mosquitos. At this point we called it a day and without having caught a single fish headed back to the car.

For the next week Dad, my brother and I itched and the welts that covered our hands, arms and faces. At night I would awaken to fierce nightmares of buzzing clouds of insects trying to get into bed with me.

CHAPTER 30

History of Hillsboro Oregon

My parents settled in Hillsboro Oregon where the majority of these events occurred after growing up and marrying in Vermont. They loved the mild climate and the greenery of the state reminded them of their home state.

Hillsboro is the county seat for Washington County in Oregon state. The court house is surrounded by beautiful fully mature sequoia trees. These trees can be spotted for many blocks in each direction and are often used for reference by those visiting.

Hillsboro is 14 miles west of Portland Oregon located in the Tualatin Valley. Founded in 1842 and named after David Hill who was a settler and pioneer as well as a member of the provisional government of Oregon.

When our family moved to Hillsboro, it was a small town of around 5000, this has grown to a city of 103,000 people today. Much of the industry was agricultural and remained the core industry until the late 1977's when Intel and several supporting tech companies turned the area into a small version of silicon valley. As a boy it was a quiet community where we road our bikes along main street in safety and where on Sundays if you stopped and had a chat while standing in the middle of the street you would not be interrupted.

I attend elementary school at Peter Boscow, then seventh and eighth grades at Poynter Junior High. Next were two years at of high school at Hillsboro Middle School for 9th and 10th graders. When first built it was the four year high school for Hillsboro. In 1978 it was renamed JB Thomas Junior High School. The middle school is gone now and has become a sports field of the same name. The school was a confortable 6 block walk from our home on Forest Street. It was here that I made my first entrance into track and field in the discus. I would like to say I was a success but at the first meet I came in 6th place out of 6 entries. I finished the season determined to make it my last season.

Hillsboro Middle school had a large auditorium and stage where I played parts in several plays while attending school there. The basement below had a shooting range where students attended classes and learned to fire 22 caliber rifles. This was also my first unfortunate run in with bullies.

My friend Kenny and I were constantly harassed, chased and kicked by the gang of three older boys. We would often report the occurrences to the principle that did his best to catch and discipline the students.

In the spring of my 7th year it all came to a head. I was outside tossing a Frisbee with Kenny. There were lots of students out that day enjoying the sunshine. I missed the start of the fight but as Kenny related the gang leader came rushing up behind me, leaped in the air and planted both feet in my back. Not the first time but today was to be the last. As I lay on the grass he made a fatal mistake of jumping onto me. I quickly flipped him onto his back and locked his arms to his side. He spit and snarled at me making venomous remarks about my family and what he was going to do. The angry welled up into me and with no feeling of remorse I grab each ear and began banging his head repeatedly against the ground until the principle arrived and told me it was over. When I got up I looked up to see Kenny, he had each of the other gang members in a head lock even though they were much bigger than him.

The principle led the gang members away and said not a word to Kenny and I. Kenny and I were never questioned but the bullies were expelled from school. Despite the previous threats we never saw them again.

I was part of the wrestling team until 10th grade when I started to become busier in Boy Scouts and DeMolay. The training was vicious as the coach made us spend hours running up and down the bleachers. This became too much for my knees so I had no choice but to drop out mid-season.

After school I loved to drop in on my Mother where she worked across from the court house, the Masonic temple where I was a DeMolay member was on the same block. She would always take time to visit the drug store that had a soda fountain, there we would talk and enjoy a treat. After walking her back to the office I would visit the Hillsboro Hobby Store on Main Street to marvel at all the cool models. Some days I would wander into the Candy Basket candy store. They had lots of fun candies to try and made many of them on site. There was also a book store called The Book Vault where I would stop a peruse there books but the real find was the used book store in Weil Arcade. I have always been an avid reader and enjoyed this addition to the community.

Hillsboro had several parks but the Shute Park near the swimming pool was a favorite. We enjoyed playing on the swings and teeter totters. On Easter there was a huge Easter egg hunt. I remember the first time that I attended and found a large chocolate Easter bunny, this is before I had glasses so I was operating at a disadvantage. I showed it to Mom and Dad who said I needed to share it with my younger brother who neatly chomped off the ears and heads with a single bite. On 4th of July they had a carnival and fireworks. This would later be moved to the fairgrounds.

Hillsboro had a main street where most of the business were located though a few blocks away was Tualatin Valley Highway nick named TV Highway and businesses were growing up quickly stretching from East and West.

The East end was the Hillsboro Swimming pool where my father took us during the summers for swimming lessons. The pool was not heated but I didn't know the difference until we tried out the Beaverton Swimming pool that was enclosed and heated. There was also the A&W Drive in where you could sit in your car, order your food and eat it there in your car. The drive-in also had several large memorable plastic statues of a family enjoying their burgers.

The fairgrounds are north east of down town where we enjoyed fairs and carnivals. On the fourth of July just there were large fireworks displays that we could see from our house. This is also while Master Councilor for Hillsboro DeMolay we enjoyed lucrative business. We purchased a corn dog truck where we made thousands of dollars over the fourth of July selling corn dogs two for a dollar. Unfortunately this was not to continue as the managers of the property at the insistence of the other vendors forced us to raise our prices to three dollars per corn dog. We took the hint and sold the trailer as sales were very poor at the higher price.

Starting in June the crops of strawberries would be ready to harvest. The farmers would send out there buses and we with our sack lunches in hand head to the fields to pick pallets of berries. My first time was at 10 years old and did not go all that well but the farmer was patient and helpful. At the time I was lucky to pick 2-3 flats earning four dollars. A couple of years later I was picking 10 flats a day. The work required bending over or kneeling in the sun. Mom purchases us some straw hats that kept the sun off but we also earned money by renting the hats out in exchange for a flat of berries.

While in college I would pick berries for extra money. I remember one place where I picked 20 flats in one day. I was told that I should challenge myself to beat a woman named Greta. So each day I would pick faster and faster only to learn she had surpassed me. On my last day I put my head down and picked furiously, I out picked the card witch only had space for 40 flats as I was cheered by my row partner. I hit 45 flats that day and the farmer came to thank me for getting his berries into the processor and to also let me know I had beat Greta, finally. He then looked at me with a grin and related that Greta and her 5 teenagers all punched the same car. Funny, very funny Mr. Farmer.

CHAPTER 31

Epilogue

I finished my Eagle scout at 17 barely making the age 18 cut off. For the ceremony my Aunt Ann made a beautiful cake with the Eagle Scout emblem decorating the top.

Upon completing Eagle Scout my parents allowed me to join DeMolay. DeMolay is a boy's organization associated with the masonic temple and similar to Jobs Daughters or Rainbow for girls. Several of my friends were members of DeMolay and had been asking me to join for months.

I rose quickly in the ranks of DeMolay starting with an appointment as a state District Representative. The following year I joined the state officer as the State Senior Deacon. We had fun for those two years travelling around the state of Oregon meeting other young men and promoting the organization.

Especially fun were all the large dances. Not like High School dances where no one dances, at our dances everyone danced to either a DJ or a live band. It was all in good fun and thoroughly enjoyable.

One night while returning home from Eugene on the I5 freeway. We saw a huge explosion on the other side of the freeway and without hesitation pulled to the side of the road. We were still dressed in our tuxedo's witch is standard garb for state officers. Wen jumped from the car and crossed the center meridian then the oncoming lanes of traffic where a two door sedan was on fire. The trunk region of the car was on fire and we spied people sitting in the front seats.

I pulled the unconscious driver from the car while my friend opened the door on the passenger side to pull out the other unconscious man. During this time the flames grew higher as we turned back to check on the passenger in the rear seat. He was frantically try to get out so we reached in through the open windows and bodily heaved him up and out. We dragged all three of them clear of the car. I started to check them over to see if they were breathing, at this point I could hear sirens in the distance.

A man raced up and stated he was a doctor so we pulled back and stood a few feet away. I turned to look at the car and it was totally engulfed in flames. The rescue squad arrived and started to care for the three men and we stood off to the side still in our tuxedos. Eventually the police asked us to disperse. This was fine by us, we didn't need any rewards or accolades, we took action because it was the right thing to do.

The next day I check the local paper and there read how the fellow in the back seat had pulled his two friends out of the burning car. We had a good chuckle knowing that he had been in no shape to do anything.

During this time the volcano Mount Saint Helens erupted in Washington State. We could see the ash plume from 50 miles away as it rose up into the atmosphere. In Hillsboro we had about 8 inches of dust fall. It was light and easily stirred up by the wind or passing cars. For many days we operated in a virtual fog of ash. When it started to rain the ash absorbed the water and became heavy weighing down roofs. I worked for my father during this period clearing the ash off of homes so that the roofs would not collapse.

I finished my time in DeMolay and Boy Scouts then headed off the college at Oregon State University where I would study to be a Mechanical Engineer. I was entering a whole new adventure in my life that would lead to working a regular jobs, marriage and fatherhood.